Heart and Soul

Heart and Soul

Ted Stuckey

ISBN-13: 9780578480138 (paperback)

Typeset by Amnet Systems.

Are you at peace and calm in your life? Are you filled with hope for a better future? Is your life filled with fear, doubts and uncertainty? Let me fill your heart with inspiration and encourage you to find a love, a peace and a joy unlike anything you have ever known. His name is Jesus Christ and He wants and desires a personal relationship with you. Come join me in discovering who God really is.

Contents

Introduction

I AM A COMMON ORDINARY man, who for 53 years has struggled all my life as a non-believer in God. That all changed just under two years ago when by God's grace He filled my heart with a love and peace unlike anything I have ever known. His presence and the power of the Holy Spirit within me has put me on an amazing journey that has me in reverent awe of God, the Father and His son our Lord and Savior Jesus Christ.

Most if not all people do have some degree of knowledge of God just by the splendor, beauty and majesty of the world that we live in. We have some understanding of Him through our senses by experiencing this world and the life we live by seeing, hearing, tasting, touching and smelling. We also use our minds to think, ponder and utilize our brains to try and understand why things are the way they are, and to make sense out of living in this often-chaotic world.

There has to be a reason, a cause, a purpose for all of this. Why do we exist? Where did we come from? Why is it we are the only planet in all the known universe teeming with life?

I am not a pastor, minister, preacher, or a theologian. In fact, most of my life, I never opened a bible, did much of any praying and truly just went about trying to live my life without God in it. I considered myself a Christian, but never truly believed in God. In a word, I was a hypocrite, pretending to be a believer.

I must also truly say I don't consider myself a writer, but more of a messenger of God, who has called me to do this. It is only through the power of the Holy Spirit that enables me to do this. He wants me to share my struggles in life as a non-believer turned believer, so that I can inspire other lost souls to draw near to the Lord and experience the Joy, Peace and Love that He has given to me.

Most of all, the ideas and words written in this book come from the power of the Holy Spirit who gives me the courage and the strength to put it all down on paper. I am deeply humbled, astonished and in reverent awe over the power that dwells within me.

The burning passion deep within my heart and soul compels me to speak and spread His words of truth, love, grace and peace. The hope and joy within in me wants to share this strong faith and trust I have in the greatness and Holiness of God the Father Almighty.

Never in my wildest dreams could I have ever imagined the Joy and Peace that drawing near to Christ brings to one's life. God's greatest desire is to have each of us in a personal relationship with Him, and to be our God, and to help us through whatever difficulties life throws at us. Not only with the personal relationship we can have with Him here in this life but to share His glory with His greatest promise of living with Him forever in everlasting life.

I have a hunger and a thirst so intense that I devote my whole heart, mind and soul in reading and studying His holy words of truth. I meditate, pray and rejoice daily in His Word and in His teaching. I just can't seem to get enough!!

While I have only been a true believer for a little less than two years, I continue to learn and grow stronger in my faith day by day.

I pray that you will read the pages of this book with an open heart and an open mind. My hope is while reading that you will discover the Love, Truth, Joy and Peace only Christ our Lord can provide!!

My Amazing Journey

MY WIFE PASSED AWAY ON November 30, 2015 due to pancreatic cancer. Because my heart was hurting, I made a commitment to myself to start reading her devotional books, hoping to heal my broken heart. She was a woman with a great deal of faith, and I was not, so I felt it could help me ease the pain of losing her.

I was a hypocrite for 53 years and was a pretend believer in Christ. I attended church earlier in my life, so I knew the **Lord's prayer** and I also knew the **Serenity Prayer**. My wife wrote her entire funeral service, so I also read that as part of my healing process.

I also started praying, asking her for forgiveness, since I was away from home a great deal as an over the road truck driver. Over time, I also started asking God for forgiveness, even though I still was a non-believer. I memorized the **"Lord make me an instrument of your peace"** prayer, which I found in one of her books. The **"Lord is my Shepherd"** prayer was also found in one of her books, so I memorized that as well.

I wasn't reading the bible at all, I just kept reading these devotionals and saying these prayers, almost daily and then, 15 months later it happened. While driving my truck in Wisconsin, God's grace filled my heart with love, and I felt the presence of the Holy Spirit fill my entire being. Words cannot describe the sheer joy of that moment. I had a radiant, warm feeling deep inside my soul and at that moment, I became a true believer in God the Father Almighty and His Son, our Lord and Savior Jesus Christ. Tears rolled down my eyes, and I stopped the truck just to reflect on what had just happened. I was ecstatic, amazed, astonished at the peace, calm and joy I felt at that moment. I was in reverent awe and wonder.

Since that amazing moment in April 2017, I have not stopped reading, meditating, praying and filling my heart with His truth, love, wisdom and the incredible promises of His Word. I literally have a hunger and a passion that has not stopped since that life changing moment. I long to share my faith and the hope that is in me with others, so they too, can have the same peace, joy, calm and contentment that I am experiencing.

In simple terms, here are the steps I followed for 15 months, before ever reading a bible, before God's grace filled my heart with love and I became a true believer.

1. I made a commitment to do this daily, to ease my broken heart.

2. I read a page or two out of a devotional book every day. (Not whenever I felt like it.)

3. I would Pray the Lord's Prayer (**Matt. 6:9-13**), or the Serenity Prayer, or the Lord Make me an Instrument of Your Peace Prayer, or The Lord is my Shepherd Prayer, **(Psalm 23)**

4. I would read my wife's funeral service. (Maybe twice a month or so)

Lord Make me an Instrument of Your Peace Prayer
(not found in scripture)
Lord, Make me an instrument of your peace;
Where there is hatred, let me sow love;
Where there is injury, pardon;
Where there is doubt, faith;
Where there is despair, hope;
Where there is darkness, light;
Where there is sadness, joy.
O divine Master, grant that I may not so much seek to be consoled, as to console; to be understood, as to understand; to be loved as to love; For it is in giving that we receive; it is in pardoning that we are pardoned; and it is in dying that we are born to eternal life.

Serenity Prayer
God grant me the serenity to Accept
the things I cannot change, the
Courage to change the things
I can and the Wisdom to
Know the difference

The Lord is My Shepherd (Psalm 23)
The Lord is my shepherd; I shall not want
He makes me to lie down in green pastures;
He leads me beside still waters.
He restores my soul;
He leads me in the path of righteousness

For His name's sake.
Yea, though I walk through the
Valley of the shadow of death,
I will fear no evil; For You are with me;
Your rod and staff, they comfort me.
You prepare a table before me
In the presence of my enemies;
You anoint my head with oil;
My cup runs over.
Surely goodness and mercy
Shall follow me, all the days
Of my life; and I will dwell in the
House of the Lord forever.

These were quite honestly the only things I was doing before that glorious life changing moment when I became alive with the presence of the Holy Spirit and I became a true believer. Of course, now, I would certainly encourage reading God's words of truth as found in all of scripture. (as outlined in Chapter 11, Spiritual Growth) Pray always and often as it helps you draw near to the Lord.

CHAPTER 1

Creation and Why We Exist

WHY DO WE EXIST? WHERE did we come from? Everything has a beginning and so it was and so it will be. We will begin with a definition of Creation: Creation shall be defined as **something** or **someone** who has created all things, both non-living and living, in all our known universe and the world we live in from nothing that had never existed before.

There are only two schools of thought as it relates to creation and how we came to exist.

The finite wisdom of man through Science versus the infinite wisdom of God

An event of Something--as opposed to--Someone with great power

Science and Man say and lead us to believe that in all the known universe and all things created, non-living and living, came into existence from a colossal and gigantic explosion known as the Big Bang Theory. That out of nothing, we, and everything we know exists, because of this explosion which occurred some 16 Billion years ago. And that the earth is some 6 ½ billion years old.

We are then expected to accept and believe that out of this gigantic cosmic explosion, which generated heat in the millions of degrees Fahrenheit, that life as we know it, was created and came into existence.

How is this possible that temperatures this great could ultimately cool down and cause life to begin? Here we have a few known facts for you to think about and consider:

1. Only 4% of the known universe is visible to us, the other 96% of the universe is darkness and consists of dark matter and dark energy, but is invisible to us and to science. It's a mystery.

2. Science is yet to determine how gravity functions, nor can they explain it. It's a mystery.

3. Science is yet to explain the enormous amount of water that makes up around 70% of our planet. It's a mystery.

4. Earth is the only known planet in all the vast universe that teems with life! No other life exists in our known universe. If Earth, as represented by the dot on this sentence, could be compared to the size of the Milky Way Galaxy, which we are a part of, it would make it invisible. The Milky Way Galaxy is 100,000 light years across and just one light year is roughly 6 trillion miles. The universe contains billions of Galaxies, so the comparison is mind boggling. Our human mind is not capable of understanding the unfathomable and incomprehensible size of our universe.

5. Science only knows and has explored only about 3% of the depths of our oceans – the remaining 97% is a mystery.

There are essential 3 components that make up our physical universe: Time, Space and Matter. All matter is made of atoms which exist in all things non-living and living. Atoms are the building blocks of all matter and cannot be broken down. All matter exists in three states: liquid, solid and gas.

Science is the study of knowledge of the physical and natural world through observation and experimentation, which helps us better understand the world we live in. Many great discoveries have benefited mankind over the years and their contributions are too numerous to mention. We all benefit from the creative minds that have made our lives better.

There is truly One and only One who has created, fashioned, molded, shaped and formed all things, non-living and living in all our entire known universe. God Almighty, by the infinite power of His word, has created everything known and unknown, visible and invisible, all for His Glory and all for His pleasure.

Isaiah 43: 7 "Everyone who is called by My name. Whom I have created for My glory: I have formed him, yes I have made them."

Genesis 1:1-4 "In the beginning God created the heavens and the earth. The earth was without form, and void; and darkness was on the face of the deep. And the Spirit of God was hovering over the face of the waters. Then God said. Let there be light: and there was light."

Colossians 1:16-17 "For by Him all things were created that are in heaven and that are on earth, visible and invisible, whether thrones or dominions or principalities or powers. All things were created through Him and for Him"

It is only and I repeat, only God who has the infinite wisdom, understanding and knowledge to create all things out of nothing. God masterminded everything and it was God who created time, space, and matter. It was God who created atoms which are the building blocks of all matter.

It was God who created light out of nothing but darkness. It was God who created gravity and has the earth spinning at precisely 1000 MPH. Amazing how it takes the earth exactly 24 hours to make one complete revolution giving us day and night. Just as God intended it to do.

Genesis 1:5 "God called the light Day, and the darkness He called Night. So, the evening and the morning were the first day (of His creation).

Make no mistake about it, God Almighty is the Creator and Maker of everything non-living and living and we are His creatures. God not only is the Creator but He continually, since the beginning of time, sustains, directs and controls His creation to work harmoniously and with all things. Without God's active involvement with all things, we would no longer exist nor would the known universe.

My friends, for years, this is what prevented me from being a true believer in God Almighty. It was simply my trust in believing in the wisdom of men and science and not in the power, truth and wisdom of God. It was my disbelief that what was said about creation in Genesis was just not possible. As I said earlier, I didn't read the Bible, I learned by just hearing about creation from scripture read during church.

Isaiah 45:12 "I have made the earth. And created man on it. I--My hands--stretched out the heavens. And all their host I have commanded."

John 1: 1-5 "In the beginning was the Word, and the Word was with God, and the Word was God. He was in the beginning with God. All things were made through Him, and without Him nothing was made that was made. In Him was life, and the life was the light of men. And the light shines in the darkness, and the darkness did not comprehend it."

It was only when God's grace filled my heart with His love, that I became a true believer, and began reading and studying the Bible. You will never become a true believer until you spend time in the truth and the power of God's word as written in the Holy Bible.

Belief in God comes from the heart and trusting completely in the knowledge, wisdom and truth that comes through His word. The Holy Bible is the absolute standard of truth and authority for all to read, study and understand the world we live in and how to live our lives for Him, through Him, and with Him.

Let me leave you with these verses to ponder and think about. **Isaiah 40:21-22** "Do you not know? Have you not heard? Has it not been told you from the beginning? Have you not understood since the earth was founded? He sits enthroned above the circle of the earth, and its people are like grasshoppers. He stretches out the heavens like a canopy, and spreads them out like a tent to live in." NIV

CHAPTER 2

Miracles

GAINING A PROPER PERSPECTIVE ON why and how we exist is crucial to understanding Who God is, What He has done for us and continues to do for us on a daily basis. It is very clear to me, since I read a lot of books, besides the Bible, that many people believe in the wisdom of men and that creation is not how God says it is, as written by Moses in the book of Genesis. My hope is that this chapter can shed light and help people get passed this deception and their non-belief .

The biggest problem I see, is the same problem I had as a non-believer for over 53 years. We approach God, the Bible and hearing His word with an intellectual mind and aren't opening up or using our hearts and souls with God. Without using the heart and soul, we spend no time reading His word and become blind to His truth and love. Since we can't accept what is said in the very first book of the Bible, we have difficulty accepting any of the other books of the Bible. We just can't see or experience His Love and His truth, so just drift away.

Miracles shall be defined as: An event which the forces of nature cannot explain, including the natural powers of man, cannot of themselves produce, and must, therefore require supernatural power or intervention.

We see miracles every day from what was created, yet don't give them a second thought. We don't consider or appreciate the beauty, the glory and the wonders that God has given us to enjoy and use. We become unaware of our surroundings and pay little attention to God's glory and blessings He provides daily. We instead focus our attention to all the work; tasks and struggles we encounter from day to day. **We get so busy just trying to survive that we forget how to live!**

Isaiah 55: 10,11 "For as the rain comes down, and the snow from heaven, and do not return there, but water the earth, and make it bring forth and bud. That it may **give seed** to the sower and **bread** to the eater. So shall My word be that goes forth from My mouth; It shall not return to me void, but it shall accomplish what I please." (emphasis mine)

Romans 1: 20 "For since the creation of the world, God's invisible qualities --His eternal power and divine nature-- have clearly been seen, being understood from what has been made, so that people are without excuse."

In the natural physical world, we see miracles in the beauty of the sunrise, the splendor of a sunset, a gentle rain, a cool breeze. The tall grass waving in the wind. The seasons: Spring, Summer, Fall and Winter. The beauty of mountains, lakes, rivers, streams and the sound of waves on the beach. The twinkling of the stars filling the night sky. The splendid colors of flowers and the vibrant colors of the leaves in the fall. Forests and waterfalls. The sweet taste of fruit and the fresh air that we breathe. Thunder and lightning. All to God's glory and for us to enjoy, use and be thankful for. These are the blessings and miracles our heavenly Father has given to us. Just a few of the many blessings God gives us.

Psalm 104: 24 "O Lord, how manifold are your works! In wisdom You have made them all. The earth is full of your possessions."

Psalm 40: 5 "Many, Oh Lord my God, are Your wonderful works, which you have done; And your thoughts toward us cannot be recounted to You in order."

Ecclesiastes 3: 1 "To everything there is a season. A time for every purpose under heaven."

Let us now consider all the miracles of the numerous living creatures in the natural world that were created by God's unsearchable and infinite wisdom. How is it possible that we have such an abundance of life? How is it that someone can be so blind to the wonders and miracles that exist daily? Plants, trees animals, reptiles, birds, insects, amphibians and all the fish. There are over 1,500,000 living species known (estimate) on our planet with still more being discovered on a yearly basis still.

According to a science article, we have over 950,000 species of insects, 10,000 species of birds, 30.000 species of fish, 8200 species of reptiles, 5400 species of mammals, and 6200 species of amphibians. We have over 297,000 plant species including mosses, algae, mushrooms etc. I didn't list them all but just wanted to show mindboggling numbers. A lot of microscopic organisms not included in this list, which some say would get the total number of living species anywhere from 2 million to 35 million species on our planet.

I was blind to all of this, never really thought much about it, nor considered any of this, just like many of you reading this book. Mark this down, highlight it and let it sink in to your heart, your mind and your soul: **We are not here on this earth by some random accident from a gigantic cosmic explosion, nor have we evolved from single organisms that could never have survived the extreme heat. We exist as does everything else on this planet because God created and made it so!!!**

Genesis 1: 29 "And God said: "See, I have given you every herb that **yields seed** which is on the face of the earth, and every tree whose fruit **yields seed; to you it shall be food**." (emphasis mine)

Genesis 1: 30 "Also, to every beast of the earth, to every bird of the air, and **to everything** that creeps on the earth, **in which there is life**, I have given every green herb **for food**"; and it was so." (emphasis mine)

These two verses apply to every living creature on our planet, including His greatest miracle and creation: **Us!** Pay particular attention to the 3 key phases within each verse, **"that yields seed"** and **"to you it shall be food"** and **"to everything in which there is life"** (emphasis mine)

God's divine plan not only in creating all of this, but in making sure He would sustain us and all living things through reproduction and new life, is incomprehensible, inconceivable and light years away from human understanding and knowledge. Every living creature, from insects, plants, trees, birds, animals, fish, and mankind, reproduce so that the cycle of life continues ! All this by a random chance ? I think not !

He has further given us light in the form of energy and sends rain to make plants grow, which not only feeds living creatures, but the plants take up Co2 in exchange for providing and producing oxygen for the air that we breathe. The cycle of life is a true miracle and designed by God's infinite wisdom and knowledge. Nothing could possibly have come up with such a complex diverse system of working in harmony within all of nature.

The greatest miracle and achievement of God's creation by far is the creation of mankind. In all God's glory He created us in His image and in His likeness. He gave man dominion over all the other creatures that He had created. He blessed man and commanded that both female and male be fruitful and multiply and subdue it. He further instructed Man to tend the garden that God had created and made.

Genesis 1: 27 "So God created man in His own image; in the image of God, He created him, male and female, He created them."

Genesis 2: 7 "And the Lord God formed man of the dust of the ground, and breathed life into his nostrils, the breath of life; and man became a living being."

Genesis 2: 16 "Then the Lord God took the man and put him in the Garden of Eden to tend and keep it."

To help us understand the working miraculous wonders of the human body let me show you several facts that most people don't ever really think about, let alone, be in wonderous awe of what God has given us.

Miracles of our heart as taken from a medical journal:

1. The heart pumps blood to 75 trillion cells in the body

2. Everyday your heart (which has its own electrical supply) generates enough energy to drive a truck 20 miles.

3. The heart pumps 2000 gallons a day. Every minute it pumps 1.5 gallons

4. The heart beats roughly 100,000 times in a 24-hour day.

5. The heart pumps blood through 60,000 miles of blood vessels daily.

6. All the blood in your body (5-6 quarts) travels through your body once a minute.

Miracles of the Brain as taken from a medical journal:

1. The complexity of the brain is astonishing and 90 % of it is still a mystery to science; while we use all our brain, science has yet to determine how it all functions.

2. The brain can transmit 1016 impulses/second which is 30x faster than the world's fastest computer.

3. It takes 13 milliseconds for the brain to process what the eyes see.

4. Brain tissue the size of a grain of sand contains 100,000 neurons(cells) and 1 billion synapses, which is the tissue connecting cells to one another.

So much wonder and awe of the greatness and miracles throughout our bodies that God has created, designed and shaped for us to live, breath and function within the world He has created. Our eyes, ears, lungs, our skeletal system, nervous system, our hands, feet stomach and all the other internal organ functions. All this designed and working together so we can see, hear, taste, smell, and touch.

We play no part in our beating hearts, our breathing, digestive system, the temperature of our bodies, our immune system, nor in delivering vital nutrients to all cells within our bodies. So astounding, remarkable, incredible and light years away from human understanding. Let us truly pause and be grateful for what He has given us.

Let this also sink deeply into your hearts and minds, so that you can accept the truth of our heavenly creator and how and why we exist. Let us remove the blindfolds that prevent us from seeing the miracles and the glory and the splendor of God.

Let us also contemplate the unfathomable, incomprehensible, wisdom and knowledge that God alone possesses. Let us all be filled with wonder and awe over His greatness and power to create all of this out of nothing.

Hear these words of truth and let them fill your heart and soul.

Isaiah 44: 24 "I am the Lord who makes all things, who stretches out the heavens all alone, who spreads abroad the earth by Myself."

Isaiah 40:13-14 "Who has directed the Spirit of the Lord? Or as His counselor has taught Him? With whom did He take counsel, and who instructed Him and taught Him in the path of justice? Who taught Him knowledge and showed Him the way of understanding?"

John 14: 6 For as Jesus said "I am the way, the truth and the life. No one comes to the Father except through Me."

CHAPTER 3

Sin and the Fall of Mankind

As I STATED EARLIER, THE reason I was a lost soul for 53 years, was my disbelief in what I was hearing during church services about creation. Again, it bears repeating that I trusted in man's wisdom as opposed to the wisdom of God. Furthermore, just like many of you, I had already based my beliefs on what I saw in the physical world. I had already determined that I would pursue what the pleasures of the world had to offer.

Ignorant and foolish, I believed in the deception and lies that Satan offered as a better way to live. Of course, all those years, I didn't view it that way. I was blind to the truth and was going by what I could see, not by what I was hearing and could not see.

Simply put, the pleasures and desires of this world were my reality. Is it possible that you too have been blinded to see the truth?

John 12: 40 "He has blinded their eyes and hardened their hearts, lest they should see with their eyes, lest they should understand with their hearts and turn, so that I should heal them."

Isaiah 6: 9,10 And the Lord said, "Go, and tell this people: Keep on hearing, but do not understand; Keep on seeing, but do not perceive, Make the heart of this people dull, and their eyes heavy, and shut their eyes; Lest they see with their eyes, and hear with their ears, an understand with their heart and return and be healed."

The definition of Sin simply put is: The disobedience and rebellion against the moral character of God in actions, thoughts and attitudes. Anything that does not please God or place Him as the absolute authority in truth, goodness, righteousness and Justice.

God is sovereign over all things created and is the Creator and the lawgiver over all His creation. He alone determines what is right and wrong. He alone determines what is fair and unfair. He alone determines what is good and bad. He alone determines life and death.

There are many verses through all of scripture that speak truth and give us knowledge of what is sin and evil in the eyes of God.

Proverbs 6: 16-19 "These six things the Lord hates, Yes, seven are an abomination to Him: A proud look, A lying tongue, Hands that shed innocent blood, A heart that devises wicked plans, Feet that are swift in running to evil, A false witness who speaks lies, And one who sows discord among brethren."

Mark 7: 20-23 For Jesus said: "What comes out of a man, that defiles a man. For from within, out of the heart of men, proceed evil thoughts, adulteries, fornications, murders, thefts, covetousness, wickedness, deceit, lewdness, an evil eye, blasphemy, pride, foolishness. All these evil things come from within and defile a man."

Romans 1: 25 "Who exchanged the truth of God for a lie and worshipped and served the creature rather than the creator. "

Matthew 12: 30 For Jesus said: "He who is not with Me is against Me, and he who does not gather with Me scatters abroad" See other verses (**James 3:16, 1 John 2:4, Romans 1: 28-32)**

We most certainly live in a fallen, broken world and have all inherited the sin that that can be traced back to God's first humans created in Adam and Eve. They were perfectly created full of God's righteousness, goodness and His divine love. They knew no evil until God had commanded them to not eat the forbidden fruit from the tree of the knowledge of good and evil.

Genesis 2: 16,17 And the Lord commanded the man saying, "Of every tree of the garden you may freely eat; but of the tree of the knowledge of good and evil you shall not eat, for in the day that you eat of it, you shall surely die."

How much clearer could God have been with this verse? Why do you find this so difficult to understand? What will it take to open your heart to the reason we live in a world full of hate, lies and deception? Who will you trust?

I will use a summary of **Genesis 3: 1-5** using the dialogue between the serpent (Satan) and Eve. The serpent asked Eve "Has God indeed said, you shall not eat of every tree in the garden?" to which Eve replies, "We can eat from all the fruit in the garden but not the fruit in the midst of the garden lest we shall die." Serpent replies back "You will not surely die, for God knows that if you eat of it, you will be like God, knowing evil and good."

Mark this down as to why we all live in Sin. Satan's deception and lies convinced Eve that she would **BE LIKE GOD** and know evil and good. In other words, rather than obey God, we could be in control of our own lives and do whatever pleased us. We need not depend and obey God because we would be like God. We would just depend upon ourselves and don't need God or anyone else to tell us what to do with our lives.

Now of course, Eve disobeyed God's command and took the fruit and gave Adam some and they both ate. Because they both disobeyed the Lord's command, He put a curse on them and all of mankind, as well as all the rest of creation. He further made a promise to Satan that He would plant a seed in Eve that would bruise his head and that He, Satan, would bruise His heel.

Genesis 3: 15 And the Lord said to Satan: "I will put enmity between you and the woman, and between your seed and her **seed**; He shall bruise your head, and you shall bruise His heel." (emphasis mine)

God's whole plan of salvation and His greatest promise to mankind was that He would bring Jesus Christ, His Son (the **seed**) into the world to redeem it and forgive us for our Sins and disobedience to His commands. The whole Bible is the story and history of Jesus Christ coming into the world to save it from sin and destruction.

The whole birth of Sin and death started with the very first humans placed on earth and some 4000 years later, continues today. For many, who can't accept this first book of the Bible, will never come to truly understand much less believe in our Lord and Savior Jesus Christ. All of God's words from Genesis to Revelation are written for our benefit so that we can gain the knowledge, the truth, the grace and the Divine Love He has for those who truly believe in Him.

To help us understand this devious creature who brought on the temptation to Eve to disobey God's command and sin, we go to the book of Ezekiel and Isaiah. It is here we get an idea that Lucifer was in fact an angel of God, who was created perfect and blameless until he rebelled and sinned against God.

Ezekiel 28: 14-16 "You were an anointed guardian cherub, I placed you; you were on the holy mountain of God; in the midst of the stones of fire you walked. You were blameless in your ways from the day you were created, till unrighteousness was found in you. In the abundance of your trade, you were filled with violence in your midst and you sinned; so, I cast you as a profane thing from the mountain of God, and I destroyed you, O guardian cherub." ESV

Isaiah 14: 12-14 "How you are fallen from heaven, O Lucifer, son of the morning! How you are cut down to the ground, you who weakened the nations! For you have said in your heart: I will ascend into heaven; I will exalt my throne above the stars of God; I will also sit on the mount of the congregation on the farthest sides of the north; I will ascend above the heights of the clouds; I will be like the Most High."

Luke 10: 18 And Jesus said: "I saw Satan fall like lightning from heaven. "

Ephesians 6: 10-12 "Finally my brethren, be strong in the Lord and in the power of His might. Put on the whole armor of God, that you may be able to stand against the wiles of the devil. For we do not wrestle against flesh and blood, but against principalities, against powers, against the rulers of darkness of this age, against spiritual hosts of wickedness in the heavenly places."

Pride, arrogance and jealousy caused Satan to rebel against God thinking he had the power to do so. He wanted **to be like God**, in fact. **above God** so He was cast out of heaven.

During Jesus' ministry and teaching, He admonished the powerful Pharisees for their lack of faith and hardened hearts. Everything was done externally for show on the outside to show people how righteous they were, and the true love of God was not in their heart.

John 8: 42-43 And Jesus said: "Why do you not understand My speech? Because you are not able to listen to My word. You are of your father, the devil, and the desires of your father you want to do. He was a murderer, from the beginning and does not stand in the truth, because there is no truth in him. When he speaks a lie, he speaks from his own sources, for he is a liar and the father of it."

Let us be reminded of the original ten commandments as a quick refresher for readers who have forgotten them or have never heard of them. It shall be in more of quick summary form and taken from the book of **Deuteronomy 5: 7-21**

Ten Commandments
You shall have no other God's before Me
You shall not have or make idols nor shall you bow
down or serve them

You shall not take the name of the Lord your God in vain
You shall observe the Sabbath day and keep it holy
You shall honor your father and your mother
You shall not murder
You shall not commit adultery
You shall not steal
You shall not bear false witness against your neighbor
You shall not covet anything that belongs to others

Now of course, 3400 years ago and in the days of Moses, there were many Pagan Gods that people worshipped and served. Today, while we may not worship statues, we have an enormous number of idols in our lives and the word for this is **IDOLATRY**. Everyone worships something-- from sports hero's to celebrities, rock stars, models, status, power, money, work, possessions, cars, houses, cabins, jewelry, clothes, sex, kids, wife's, husbands, boats, art, movies – etc.

We either worship and serve ourselves, our possessions, our careers, and money or we worship, love and serve God. As Jesus said in **Matthew 6: 24** "No one can serve two masters; for either he will hate the one and love the other, or else he will be loyal to the one and despise the other. You cannot serve God and mammon (riches)" emphasis mine.

We all have a master that holds us as a slave and that is what we serve, love and worship. We are either a slave to sin and idolatry or we are a slave to God serving Him in love and obedience. Placing anything of value in your life **above God is Sin, pure and simple.** Now after reading this you may say, this isn't so, you may be thinking to yourself, well I follow these commands and live a decent, honest, law abiding and good life.

You may also think and believe since Christ died for your sins you have been forgiven and can go about living your life any way you see fit. If you have not found the love of Jesus Christ in your heart and confessed that He is your Lord and Savior, then you are still under the power of the wickedness and evil in this world.

You are choosing to live your way over God's way and that my friends is rebellion and disobedience to God.

I was a hypocrite for 53 years and that easily could be where you are as well. I too was trying to live my life on anything other than for God. I was in control of my life, chasing after material possessions and worldly pleasures. In truth, I was a fake, pretending to be a Christian and not a true believer in Christ.

It was only when God's grace and love came into my heart that has completely transformed and changed my whole life. I can truly and beyond any doubt say that Jesus Christ is my number one priority in my life. I no longer have a desire to live my life in the flesh but am living my life through the Holy Spirit that dwells within me. I am truly walking in the light and have a very personal relationship with God. He has given me a Peace and Joy unlike anything I have ever known. When you draw near to the Lord, He will draw near to You.

James 4: 8 "Draw near to God and He will draw near to you. Cleanse your hands, your sinners; and purify your hearts, you double minded."

In regard to our inherent desire for sin, we must remember that everyone is a sinner. See (**Romans 3: 9-18**) As human beings we all will sin, for we have inherited this from the very beginning of time and is part of our nature to do so.

The difference being that a non-believer is consistently driven by the desires of the world - greed, anger, self-seeking, arrogance, envy, pride and lust of the flesh, with no desire to have God in their lives. They are in control of their own lives.

True believers, on the other hand, are driven by the desires of the Holy Spirit so don't have continuous sin. True believers have submitted control of their lives to Christ. They pursue the desires or fruit of the Spirit (**Galatians 5:22**) and keep their hearts and minds firmly fixed on Christ.

I will tell you there are only two ways to come into a relationship with our heavenly Father.

1. Through prayer and meditation

2. Allowing God's words of truth to speak to your heart through the Holy Scripture.

Your must open your heart and mind to the message of truth and love and allow it to soak into your entire being. This is God's greatest command:

Matthew 22: 37-40 For as Jesus said; "You shall love the Lord your God with all your heart, with all your soul and with all your mind. This is the first and great commandment. And the second one is like it; You shall love your neighbor as yourself. On these two commandments hang all the Law and the Prophets."

This same commandment was given to God's people over 3400 years ago by Moses in **Deuteronomy 6:5** So you can see how

God has always commanded His people to Love Him above everything else in their life.

We must remember that evil and sin is continually working nonstop to prevent you from allowing Christ to come into your life. His power is great, and you will not be able to resist his power on your own. You must depend on God to help you and strengthen you to fight His wicked scheming ways. His attacks are relentless because he knows that when you have Christ in you that he is powerless. He preys on your weaknesses and continues to keep your blind to the truth about God.

1 Peter 3: 5 "Be sober, be vigilant; because your adversary the devil walks about like a roaring lion, seeking whom he may devour."

Romans 8: 5-7 "For those who live according to the flesh set their minds on the things of the flesh, but those who live according to the Spirit, the things of the Spirit. For to be carnally minded is death, but to be Spiritually minded is life and peace. Because the carnal mind is enmity against God; for it is not subject to the law of God, nor indeed can be."

In conclusion, let us consider these two verses which I think can help you understand where you are at when it comes to the desires of your heart as it relates to the sin in your life. As a sinner myself, it helps to read these two verses to gain knowledge of the truth and focused on Christ. and away from evil.

1 John 2: 15 "Do not love the world or the things in the world. If anyone loves the world, the love of the Father is not in him."

1 John 2: 16,17 "For all that is in the world - the lust of the flesh, the lust of the eyes, and the pride of life – is not of the Father but is of the world."

Attributes of God

WE WILL NOW TURN TO the characteristics of God which further helps us increase our knowledge and understanding of who God is and what God continues to do for us daily. All those years of unbelief was mostly due to my rejection of just hearing about God. All those years with no real desire in my heart to get to know God. How foolish, blind and ignorant I was in believing I could and would choose my own way.

In this chapter, I hope to answer these four questions: Who God really is? What is God like? What kind of God is He? Will knowing more about God help us discover and encourage us to learn more about God?

These characteristics of God are found throughout all of scripture and can be used to increase our present level of awareness or lack thereof. The first six on this list are characteristics that God alone possesses. While I used numbers on listing many of God's attributes, they are to not to be interpreted as degrees or levels of importance. Nor is this an exhaustive list of God's characteristics.

1. **God is Self-existing.** He is Infinite, eternal and has always existed. He has never been created or come into being. **Exodus 3: 14** God spoke to Moses and said; "I AM WHO I AM. "Scripture teaches that God needs nothing from creation to exist. **Acts 17: 24-25** "The God who made the world and everything in it, being Lord of heaven and earth, does not live in shrines made by man, nor is he served by human hands, as though he needed anything, since he Himself gives to all men life and breath and everything."

   Job 41: 11 and God said, "Everything under heaven is Mine "Again in **Job 12: 10** "In God's hand is the life of every living thing and the breath of all mankind." The last sentence in **Colossians 1: 16** "All things were created through Him and for Him." **Revelation 1: 8** The Lord said; "I am the Alpha and the Omega, the Beginning and the End. Who is and who was and who is to come, the Almighty" Many other verses in the Bible speak to God's existence and the creator of all.

2. **God is Unchangeable (Immutable).** God never changes in His being, in His purposes, in His promises, or in His perfection. **Malachi 3: 6** "For I am the LORD, I do not change." In **James 1: 17** James reminds us that "all perfect gifts are from above and there is no variation or shadow of turning" We can rest assured that His blessings and gifts will continue unchanged as it is the nature of God to do so.

   Psalm 102: 27 "You are the same and Your years will never end." **Isaiah 46: 9-11** "I am God and there is no other; I am God, and there is none like Me, declaring the end from the beginning, and from ancient times things, not yet done," Saying , "My counsel shall stand, and I will do all My pleasure"

Isaiah 43: 10-11 "Understand that I am He. Before me there was no God formed, nor shall there be after Me. I, even, I, am the Lord, and besides Me there is no savior." God's promises are always kept and do not change.

Numbers 23: 19 "God is not a man, that He should lie, nor a son of man that He should repent. Has He said, and will He not do? or has He spoken, and will He not make it good? I have spoken, and I will bring it to pass; I have purposed, and I will do it." **Hebrews 13:8** "Jesus Christ is the same yesterday, today and forever."

3. **God is Self – Sufficient.** God never needs anything, He is totally and perfectly complete within His being. **John 5: 26** Jesus said "For as the Father has life in Himself, so He has granted the Son to have life in Himself."

All living creatures need and depend on God to provide us with air to breath, food to eat, water to drink, clothes to wear, and shelter to protect from the elements. Without any of these gifts from God, we could not exist, we could not survive. While we certainly need Him to sustain us and His creation, He needs nothing from us. **Psalm 36:9** "For with You is the fountain of life; In your light we see light."

4. **God is Omnipresent** God is present everywhere with His whole being, all at once instantly in all of creation.

God is not limited to time or space nor has no boundaries. **Ephesians 4: 6** "One God the Father of all who is above all, and through all and in you all."

Omnipresence, Omnipotence and Omniscience are the most difficult characteristics for us to comprehend as humans. We just find it hard to embrace the realm that God functions in.

A great place to look for help can be found in **Psalm 139: 6-10** "Such knowledge is too wonderful for me. It is high; I cannot attain it. Where can I go from Your Spirit? or where can I flee from your presence? If I ascend into heaven, you are there; If I make my bed in hell, behold You are there. If I take the wings of the morning, and dwell in the uttermost parts of the sea, even there Your hand shall lead me, and Your right hand shall hold me."

Jeremiah 23: 23-24 "Am I a God near at hand," says the Lord, "And not a God afar off? Can anyone hide himself in secret places, So I shall not see him? Do I not fill heaven and earth? "Deuteronomy **10: 14** "Indeed heaven and the highest heavens belong to the Lord your God, also the earth with all that is in it." **Acts 17: 28** "For in Him we live and move and have our being.

5. **God is Omniscient.** "God is all knowing and all seeing. God knows and sees all things past, present and future. God is the creator of knowledge and wisdom and He never needs to learn. **1 John 3: 20** "God is greater than our heart and knows all things."

His wisdom and knowledge is unsearchable and will never be known as stated in **Colossians 2: 2-3** "That their hearts may be encouraged, knit together in love and attaining to all riches of the full assurance of understanding, to the knowledge of the mystery of God, both of the Father and of Christ, in whom are hidden all the treasures of wisdom and knowledge."

1 Corinthians 2: 11-14 "For what man knows the things of a man except the spirit of the man which is in him? Even so no one knows the things of God except the Spirit of God. Now we have not received the spirit of the world, but the Spirit who is from God, that we might know the things that have been given freely to us by God. There things we also speak, not in words which man's wisdom teaches but which the Holy Spirit teaches, comparing spiritual things with spiritual. But the natural man does not receive the things of the Spirit of God for they are foolishness to him; nor can he know them, because they are spiritually discerned."

1 Corinthians 3: 19-20 "For the wisdom of this world is foolishness with God." For as it was written in **Job 5: 13** "He catches the wise in their own craftiness." and again in **Psalm 94:11** "The Lord knows the thoughts of the wise, that they are futile"

6. **God is Omnipotent.** God has unlimited supernatural power unlike anything known. The human mind is not even remotely possible to comprehend or conceive of the Almighty power and might that God possesses.

He can do anything He wills with no effort on His part. For just by His Word, He created all things living and non-living. **Psalm 33: 6-9** "By the word of the Lord the heavens were made, and all the host of them by the breath of His mouth. He gathers the waters of the sea together as a heap; He lays up the deep in storehouses. Let all the earth fear the Lord; let all inhabitants of the world stand in awe of Him. For He spoke, and it was done; He commanded, and it stood fast."

Hebrew 1: 2,3 "By His Son, whom He appointed heir of all things, through whom also He made the worlds; who being the brightness of His glory and the express image of His person, and upholding all things by the word of His power, when He had by Himself purged our sins, sat down at the right hand of the Majesty on high." Additional verses of His Almighty Power (**Proverbs 8: 22-31, Isaiah 44: 2, Isaiah 45: 5,6; 12,13, Isaiah 51: 15,16,**

7. **God is Faithful.** God's faithfulness is an essential part of His divine nature. His love and faithfulness to His people throughout all of scripture is clearly seen. It is the basis of our confidence and trust in Him that He will fulfill His promises as found in His words of truth. **Psalm 119: 90** "Your faithfulness endures to all generations." **2 Samuel 7: 28** "And now O Lord God, You are God and Your words are true, and You have promised this goodness to your servant."

As with all God's traits, they are all interconnected within His whole being and can not be separated out or put into separate parts. His immutability, goodness, mercy, grace, truth, righteousness, holiness, wisdom etc. are all why we place our trust in Him. **Deuteronomy 7: 9** "Therefore know that the Lord your God, He is God, the faithful God who keeps covenant and mercy for a thousand generations with those who love Him and keep His commandments."

Deuteronomy 32: 4 "He is the Rock, His work is always perfect; For all His ways are justice, A God of truth and without injustice; Righteous and upright is He." **John 17: 17** Jesus said, "Your word is truth"

God Himself is the standard and definition of truth, and truth and trust are the essence of faith and faithfulness. His faithfulness will always be there because of His great love for us.

8. **Goodness of God** is the standard and authority of goodness and moral character for us to follow and live by. He is the absolute supreme standard of good and goodness and is so worthy of our praise and admiration.

He is Holy, Sacred and is too beheld in Reverent Awe of Who He is and What He has done and continues to do for us daily.

Luke 18: 19 For Jesus said; "Why do you call Me good? No one is good but One, that is God." **Psalm 34: 8** "Oh taste and see that the Lord is good; Blessed is the man who trusts in Him." **Psalm 34: 10** "Those who seek the Lord shall not lack any good thing." **Genesis 1: 31** "Then

God saw everything that He made, and indeed it was very good." **Romans 8: 28** "And we know that all things work together for good for those who love God, to those who are called according to His purpose."

Romans 12: 2 "And do not be conformed to this world, but be transformed by the renewing of your mind, that you may prove what is that good and acceptable and the perfect will of God." **Galatians 6: 9** "Let us not grow weary while doing good, for in due season we shall reap if we do not lose heart." Additional verses (**Psalm 107: 8,9, Ps 106:1, Ps 119: 68, Ps 84: 11**)

9. **God is Love.** God's love is the essence of His entire being which flows and is connected into all of His other attributes. It was out of His great love that all things came into existence and fills Him with great joy and pleasure. Before earth and heaven were created, we were established in the mind and the heart of God.

His entire Plan from the very beginning of time and creation was for us to be His people, so that He could live with us in all of eternity. **Ephesians 1: 4,5** "He chose us in Him before the foundation of the world, that we should be holy and without blame before Him in love, having predestined us to adoption as sons by Jesus Christ to Himself, according to the good pleasure of His will."

The entire Bible is filled with God's Love from the start in Genesis to the end in Revelation. It is the story of Jesus Christ and His divine plan of salvation.

The key to life and living is all about Love. God loving us and we loving Him. I will include several here and then list other verses in the Appendix for further study. The most familiar verse is **John 3:16** "For God so loved the world that He gave His only begotten Son, that whoever believes in Him should not perish but have everlasting life."

Matthew 22: 37-40 "You shall love the Lord your God with all your heart, with all your soul, and with all your mind. This is the first and great commandment. And the second is like it; You shall love your neighbor as yourself, on these two commandments hang all the Law and the Prophets. "

10. **God is Just, and Righteous.** God is the ultimate authority of righteousness and justice and always acts in accordance with what is right and just. **Deuteronomy 32: 3-4** "Ascribe greatness to our God. He is the Rock, His work is perfect; For all His ways are justice, A God of truth and without injustice; righteous and upright is He." **Genesis 18: 25** "Shall not the Judge of all earth do, right?" **Isaiah 45: 19** "I the Lord speak righteousness, I declare things that are right."

Because God is the creator of us all and we His creatures, He has the absolute and final say on what is right, we the creatures have no say. God has set about and established moral standards and commands as to how He wants us to live.

Anything against God's moral standards are an affront to His Holiness and He is perfectly justified in whatever he deems necessary as a punishment to the wrongs committed. The wages of Sin and evil are death in the eyes of God.

Through the great sacrifice and crucifixion of His Son Jesus Christ, God has demonstrated to us that He is righteous and just. He allowed His Son to take the punishment of death for sin on behalf of all mankind due to man's inability to live sin free lives.

Romans 3: 23-26 "For all have sinned and fall short of the glory of God, being justified freely by His grace through the redemption that is in Jesus Christ., whom God set forth as a propitiation by His blood, through faith, to demonstrate His righteousness, because in His forbearance God had passed over the sins that were previously committed, to demonstrate at the present time His righteousness, that He might be just and the justifier of the one who has faith in Jesus."

Just like the country we live in, laws are established so people have what is acceptable and what is unacceptable to live in harmony and peace with one another. Without laws, people and societies would be left to do whatever they please to one another with no consequences for their actions. With crimes against laws there will always be a punishment, or a sentence imposed for their conduct.

11. **God's Mercy.** God's mercy is compassion and kindness to those who are suffering and in need of relief. **Romans 9: 15,16,18** "I will have mercy on whomever I will have mercy, and I will have compassion on whomever I will have compassion. So, then it is not of him who wills, nor of him

who runs, but of God who shows mercy. Therefore, He has mercy on whom He wills, and whom He wills He hardens." (also, in Exodus 33:19)

Without Mercy we have no hope of heaven because of disobedient hearts and deserve death, but because of the mercy of God we get life through faith in Jesus Christ.

Ephesians 2: 4,5 "God who is rich in mercy, because of His great love with which He loved us, even when we were dead in trespasses, made us alive together with Christ." Jesus speaking to the Pharisees in **Matthew 23: 23** "You have neglected the weightier matters of the law; justice and mercy and faith. These you ought to have done. without leaving the others undone."

2 Corinthians 1: 3 "Blessed be the God and Father of our Lord Jesus Christ, the Father of mercies and God of all comfort, who comforts us in all our tribulation, that we may be able to comfort those who are in any trouble, with the comfort with which we ourselves are comforted by God."

12. **God's Grace** is God's free gift to provide a sufficient means of obtaining salvation through Christ's death on the cross through faith. It is unearned or unmerited and totally a free gift of God. **Ephesians 2: 8-10** "For by grace you have been saved through faith and that not of yourselves; It is the gift of God, not of works lest anyone should boast. For we are His workmanship, created in Christ Jesus for good works, which God prepared beforehand that we should walk in them."

It is through God's great love and mercy that He grants us this free gift. This gift comes only to true believers in Christ through sincere faith in the heart. Grace comes only from God who empowers us with the Holy Spirit by regeneration for salvation.

1 Peter 1:5 "Who by God's power are being guarded through faith for a salvation ready to be revealed in the last time." It takes an open heart and a willingness to commit your life to Christ. If you are willing to spend time reading God's words of truth, praying and allowing God to speak to you through His words, you too will discover true happiness, joy and peace that only Christ can provide.

13. **God is Holy.** God's holiness is sacred, revered, adored, exalted and divine. He is the essence of purity, perfection, peace, joy, goodness, mercy, grace, righteousness and justice.

He detests evil and impurity and commands complete submission and loyalty to His supremacy. He is to be held with reverent awe and to the highest degree of honor and respect.

Jesus said in **Matthew 5: 48** "Therefore you shall be perfect, just as your Father in heaven is perfect." **1 Peter 1: 15,16** "He who called you is holy, you also be holy in all your conduct, because as it is written, be holy for I am holy."

He cannot be around or see evil, so He relies on the Holy Spirit to fight the wicked ways and forces of evil here on earth. He also through the Holy Spirit works within believers in the process of sanctification preparing us here on earth to carry out our purpose on into eternity.

2 Corinthians 7:1 "Therefore, having these promises, beloved, let us cleanse ourselves from all filthiness of the flesh and spirit, perfecting holiness in the fear of God." The fear of the Lord is to detest and hate evil as does God. **2 Corinthians 6: 16** "You are the temple of the living God. As God has said; I will dwell in them and walk among them, I will be their God, and they shall be my people." **(Ezek. 37:26)**

14. **God is Peace.** God's peace is a separation from all confusion, chaos, and conflict and is a state of serenity and tranquility unlike anything we know. God himself is the God of Peace. **Romans 15: 33** "Now the God of peace be with you." **Romans 16: 20** "And the God of peace will crush Satan under your feet shortly. The grace of our Lord Jesus Christ be with you."

Ephesians 2: 14,15 "For He himself is our peace, who has made both one, and has broken down the middle wall of separation, having abolished in His flesh the enmity, that is, the law of commandments contained in ordinances, so as to create in Himself one new man from the two, thus making peace." **1 Thessalonians 5: 23** "Now may the God of peace Himself sanctify you completely; and may your whole spirit, soul, and body be preserved blameless at the coming of our Lord Jesus Christ."

Jesus said in **John 14: 27** "Peace I leave with you, My peace I give to you; not as the world gives do I give you. Let not your heart be troubled, neither let it be afraid."

15. **God is Truth.** God is truth and the absolute standard of truth. There is no other authority of supreme divine truth found anywhere. For as Jesus said in **John 14: 6** "I am the way the truth and the life." The definition of truth in the dictionary is: what is found true in accordance with fact or reality. A fact or reality that is accepted as true. The quality or state of being true.

   The question then becomes are you a true believer in God? For if you are, the very words of God are the truth as written in all the scripture in the Holy Bible. For as Jesus said in **John 17:17** "Sanctify them by Your truth, Your word is truth." **Hebrews 6: 18** "It is impossible for God to lie."

   Psalm 12:6 "The words of the Lord are pure, like silver tried in a furnace of earth, Purified seven times. You shall keep them O Lord, You shall preserve them from this generation." Also, in **1 John 5:20** "And we know the that the Son of God has come and has given us an understanding, that we may know Him who is true; and we are in Him who is true, in His Son Jesus Christ. This is the true God and eternal life."

   In our search for knowledge in all areas of the natural and social sciences and we will discover more truth about the nature of reality. In doing so we will discover what God already knows. He is the source of all knowledge and wisdom and much of it is unsearchable. All truth is God's truth because He has created it all and will reign supreme as the ultimate authority.

Proverbs 30:5 "Every word of God is pure; He is a shield to those who put their trust in Him."

It bears repeating that what has been listed as the characteristics of God is not an exhaustive list of the many traits that God possesses. Let it further be said that we do share and can imitate and strive to obtain goodness, kindness, peace, gentleness, love, compassion, happiness, patience and joy in our lives. Only God is perfect in all these attributes

FOUNTAIN OF LIFE

CHAPTER 5

The Presence of God

GOD IS A LIVING GOD and in His infinite wisdom and love for us, has chosen out of His own free will to be actively involved with what He has created. We and all His living creatures depend entirely on this active involvement whether you choose to accept this or not.

The mere fact that you woke up this morning to see the sunrise, see your loved ones, get coffee and a bite to eat is God actively sustaining and keeping you and the rest of creation in existence.

There is no other religion in the world that can make this claim. God is present to ensure that His Divine plan of salvation continues as planned from the very beginning of time. We get a preview of what God's ultimate goal has been when we refer to Revelation as written by John in **Revelation 21: 3,4** "Behold, the tabernacle of God is with men, and He will dwell with them, and they shall be His people. God himself will be with them and be their God. And God will wipe away every tear from their eyes; there shall be no more death, nor sorrow, nor crying. There shall be no more pain, for the former things have passed away."

This is the very reason God has fashioned, molded, formed and created us. This clearly explains the why, the what and how God has been working throughout all the history of mankind to arrive at a new heaven and a new earth so He can dwell with us.

We can either reject, which most have, or accept this truth. You must have an open heart and mind to allow this to penetrate every fiber of your being.

For the very next few verses **Revelation 21:5-7** "Then He who sat on the throne said, Behold, I make all things new." And He said to me, "Write for these words are true and faithful." And He said to me, "It is done! I am the Alpha and the Omega, the Beginning and the End. I will give of the fountain of the water of life freely to him who thirsts. He who overcomes shall inherit all things, and I will be his God and he shall be My son."

Additional verses **(Levit.26: 12, Deut. 23: 14; Deut. 7:21; Ezek. 37: 27; 2 Cor. 6:16; 1 Cor. 3:16; John 1:14)** Accept these words of truth and continue to grow in your faith and understanding.

Jesus Christ, the seed which is found in the words of Moses in Genesis was the very beginning of God's plan of salvation for all of humanity.

Genesis 3:14,15 "So the Lord God said to the serpent because you have done this, I will put enmity Between you and the woman, and between your seed and her seed; He shall bruise your head, and you shall bruise His heel."

Adam and Eve failed to carry out God's plan for having them subdue and have dominion over all the world. It was their disobedience to follow His command, that God placed His curse over all creatures and cast Adam out of the garden. By their actions, they became separated from God's presence in the physical sense yet not in the spiritual sense.

As a result, Satan, the prince of darkness became the ruler of this world and is the reason many continue to reject nor accept God's ways of living and are blinded by the truth. However, He too (Satan) is under the control of God Almighty and can do nothing to stop God from reaching His final objective.

Jesus said in **Matthew 24: 35** "Heaven and earth will pass away, but My words will by no means pass away." Again, Jesus said in **Matthew 5:18** "For truly I say to you, until heaven and earth pass away, not an iota, not a dot, will pass from the Law until all is accomplished. ESV

When we become true believers in Christ and have accepted Him as our Lord and Savior, then and only then does the presence of the Holy Spirit come alive within us. When the presence of Christ is felt and firmly planted within our heart and in our mind, do we gain and find true peace, happiness and joy. Only then do we put away the desire to live in the flesh and live our lives through and for Jesus Christ in the spirit. Only then do we focus our hearts and mind on Christ.

Galatians 2:20 "I have been crucified with Christ. It is no longer I who live, but Christ who lives within me, And the life I now live in the flesh I live by faith in the Son of God, who loved me and gave Himself for me."

For Jesus said in **John 7: 37,38** "If anyone thirsts, let him come to Me and drink. He who believes in Me, as the scripture has said, Out of His heart will flow rivers of living water." **(Isaiah 12:3; 43:20; 44:3; 55:1; Deut. 8: 15)**

Proverbs 20:27 "The spirit of a man is the lamp of the Lord, Searching all the inner depths of his heart." **(1 Cor. 2: 11; James 2:26; Rom. 11:33)**

Hebrews 4:12 "For the word of God is living and powerful, and sharper than any two-edged sword, piercing even to the division of soul and spirit, and of joints and marrow, and is a discerner of the thoughts and intents of the heart."

God's presence and His ultimate plan of salvation is His intense desire for us to draw near to Him. He longs to have a personal relationship with us so that we can become part of His grand plan. He loves us dearly and wants us to become part of His family as adopted Sons and Daughters, but it requires a willingness on our part to draw near to Him. He has given us the freedom to make that choice.

God will not make the decision for us, we must actively seek it out on our own.

It was only after the death of my wife three years ago on November 30, 2015, where I started the process of healing the pain of my heart over her loss. I needed something to help the hurt inside, so out of my love for her, I made a commitment to myself and started reading some of the many devotional books she had. I kept this reading up for over 15 months and to my utter amazement in April of 2017, Jesus Christ came into my life.

It was the most glorious experience I have ever known. God's grace filled my heart with His love and it was at that moment that I became a true believer. I was filled with a joy, a peace, a calmness, beyond words. From the moment I believed, the Holy Spirit has put me on a journey that has left me speechless and in reverent awe.

The most important decision you will ever make in your life is to open your heart and your mind to the truth, love and peace of God's word and allow Him into your life!!! Discover, as I have, the unimaginable Joy that only He can and will provide.

Psalm 16: 11 "You will show me the path of life; In your presence is fullness of joy; At your right hand are pleasures forevermore."

CHAPTER 6

Glory of God

To FULLY COMPREHEND WHAT THE glory of God is, you must first completely and totally embrace not only His creation but why we exist. Without a firm understanding of why we exist you will never come into a deeper sense of who and what He does for us.

Glory shall be defined as: God's manifestation of His divine attributes, His holiness and the splendor of His excellence and supreme being.

For it was God in all His Glory who sent His one and only Son into the world to save mankind from death and destruction. **John 1:14** "And the word became flesh and dwelt among us, and we beheld His glory, the glory as of the only begotten of the Father, full of grace and truth." For as Jesus said in **John 3:17** "For God did not send His Son into the world to condemn the world, but that the world through Him might be saved."

God and God alone is deserving of this glory and the only one worthy of the highest honor possible in all of His creation. His splendor and majestic magnificence are without comparison and will be held in reverent awe and wonder.

We were created, shaped and molded all for His great pleasure and all for His great glory. **Isaiah 43:7** "Everyone who is called by My name, whom I have created for My glory; I have formed them, yes, I have made them." **Psalm 63: 2,3** "So I looked for you in the sanctuary, to see Your power and Your glory; because Your lovingkindness is better than life." **Psalm 57:5** "Be exalted, O God, above the heavens; Let your glory be above all the earth." **Psalm 42:8** "I am the Lord, that is My name; and My glory I will not give to another."

We see the glory of God in all His creation being magnified and is on full display of God's greatness. All throughout scripture the glory of God is shown.

The birth of Jesus as written in **Luke 2:14** "Glory to God in the highest, and on earth peace, goodwill toward men." This is God's greatest glory in showing the world the coming of the promised messiah that would become the King of all Kings and reign supreme among all nations. Also the prophesy by Isaiah 680 years before the death of Christ as seen in **Isaiah 40:5** "The glory of the Lord shall be revealed, and all flesh shall see it together; For the mouth of the Lord has spoken."

As seen when ministering to others we read in **1 Peter 4:11** "If anyone ministers let him do it as with the ability which God supplies, that in all things God may be glorified through Jesus Christ to whom belong the glory and the dominion forever and ever."

It is very clear throughout scripture who we are to give glory to, for He is the only one deserving of our worship and praise.

1 Corinthians 1:30,31 "Of Him you are in Christ Jesus, who became for us wisdom from God -and righteousness and sanctification and redemption - that, as it is written, He who glories, let him glory in the Lord." See also **(Jer. 9:23,24)**

God's divine plan of salvation which began in Genesis with the fall of man in Adam and His disobedience on into the sacrifice and death of Jesus on the cross was all part of God's plan from the start. **Ephesians 1: 4-9** "He **chose us in Him before the foundation of the world**, that we should be holy and without blame before Him in love. Having **predestined** us to **adoption** as sons by Jesus Christ to Himself, according to the **good pleasure of His will**, to the **praise of the glory of His grace**, by which He **made us accepted** to the Beloved. In Him we have redemption, through His blood, the forgiveness of sins, **according to the riches of His grace**. Which He made **to abound toward us** in all wisdom and prudence, having made known to us the **mystery of His will**, according to His good pleasure which He purposed in Himself." (emphasis mine in bold)

These verses are a great summary of God's greatest crown of achievement of the saving work of His son Jesus Christ on the cross to the glory of His Grace. **Ephesians 2: 6** "For by grace you have you been saved through faith, and that not of yourselves; it is the gift of God, not of works, lest anyone should boast."

This was God's' ultimate pinnacle of Salvation through the sacrifice of His Son for redemption, reconciliation and the forgiveness of sins to make us righteous and holy before God according to the riches and glory of God's grace.

Think on this, let the words of God speak to you and fill your heart so that you may understand His great love for us. Before the earth was ever created by God -- we were chosen -- predestined to adoption – according to the good pleasure of His will-- to demonstrate to the world the glory of His Grace -- according to the full richness of His grace – to abound toward us -- having made known the mystery of His will.

This remarkable grand plan not only shows His glory but the power and wisdom that God alone possesses.

The entire story of the Bible is God's autobiography and is all about Jesus and coming into the world to save humanity from sin and death. This is Jesus' true story and is all about Him and what He has done and continues to do. God planned all of this before ever creating a single atom and creating all our known universe. His unfathomable wisdom is just astounding and indeed why all Glory belongs to God.

Let me leave you all with the very own words of God as spoken through the prophet Jeremiah. **Jeremiah 9:23-24** "Let not the wise man glory in his wisdom, Let not the mighty man glory in his might, Nor let the rich man glory in his riches; But let him who glories, glory in this, That he understands and knows Me. That I Am the Lord, exercising lovingkindness, judgment, and righteousness in the earth. For in these I delight, says the Lord."

CHAPTER 7

Characteristics to Live By

THE WORLD THAT WE LIVE in is filled with a wide variety of cultures, customs, languages, political upheavals, civil disobedience, moral issues, lifestyles, philosophies, values, ethics, laws, justice and personalities. We all have different beliefs, attitudes, behaviors, how we live our lives, where we work, where we live and how to get along with others in a civilized manner.

Most of us know right from wrong because God gave us all a mind and a brain, to reason, think, ponder, meditate, attain knowledge, think and learn new skills. **Isaiah 44:2** "Thus says the Lord who made you and formed you from the womb, who will help you." **Isaiah 44:24** "He who formed you from the womb; I am the Lord, who makes all things."

We learn in one of three ways, watching or seeing how something is done, reading about how something is done and hearing about how something is done. With knowledge we must then apply it and continue through experience to become better at it. We learn-do-repeat and continue to learn better ways of doing something.

Experience is by far the best teacher. We learn by our mistakes (assuming of course that most do, but some don't), and change course to attain a better outcome. Everybody makes mistakes, it is all part of living and growing. We can't possibly know how the outcome of any decision we make will turn out. Only God has the knowledge of how things turn out in our lives. Oh, you may think you are in control, but you are not, unless you know when your time is up. This can be best described by Solomon in **Ecclesiastes 1:9** "That which has been, is what will be, that which is done is what will be done, and there is nothing new under the sun."

As it has been throughout all of history, man continues to reject and rebel against God's way of living. It is our mistaken belief that we know better than God on how best to live our lives and be in control of things. You are exactly where God has put you. He will continue to work faithfully in drawing you near to Him, but it ultimately requires a decision on your part to seek him out.

Decision making is easy when you know where your values are. Where are your values?

Do you continue to make the same mistakes over and over in your life? Are you content and happy with your life right now? There is a way to live a better life and experience a peace and joy unlike anything you have ever known. His name is Jesus Christ and He said in **John 14:6** "I am the way, the truth and the life. No one comes to the Father except through Me."

In **Romans 12** the Apostle Paul gives us characteristics that we can live by and become a better person living in the light of Christ. Paul first begins by encouraging us in Romans 12 on how to present ourselves acceptable to Christ in serving Him and to use our gifts to the benefit of helping one another in sharing our faith. **Romans 12:2** "Do not be conformed to this world, but be transformed by the renewing of your mind, that you may prove what is that good acceptable and perfect will of God."

The Apostle Paul then takes us into the how we, as Christians, are to behave in our hearts and act toward one another which is presented in the following fourteen traits taken from Romans **12: 9-21**

1. **Let love be without hypocrisy.** Love must be genuine and sincere from the heart, not fake, phony and false. Love goes way beyond just a feeling and is best described in **1 Corinthians 1:13:13**, where we learn that without love, we are nothing. We learn love bears all things, endures all things and that love never fails. Love is God's greatest commandment **Matthew 22:37-40**.

2. **Hate what is evil.** We learn that the fear of the Lord is to hate evil, along with pride arrogance, evil ways and a perverse mouth, as found in **Proverbs 8:13.** also (**Prov. 3:7; 16:6; 16:17; 4:24)**

3. **Cling to what is good.** We learn that by doing good we will not lack any good thing **Psalm 34:10. (Also Rom. 8:28; 2 Tim 2:15, Matt. 12:35)**

4. **Be kind to one another.** Kindness comes from the heart and has no room for rudeness indifference or insensitivity. Kindness is a product, the fruit of the Holy Spirit in **Galatians 5:22.** Next to Godliness, we see in; **2 Peter 1:7,** is brotherly kindness and brotherly love. The sacrifice of our Lord and Savior is the epitome of His loving kindness to all of humanity.

5. **Give one another honor and respect.** We learn to live by the Golden rule as found in **Matthew 7:12.** We respect those in authority, and before honor is humility as in **Proverbs 15:33**. We follow what Jesus spoke in **John 5:23** that all shall honor the Father and the Son above all else.

6. **Be diligent, loyal and fervent in spirit in serving the Lord.** Never lose our energy in speaking our faith and the love of the Lord to others. God is a rewarder of those who seek him out with all diligence **Hebrew 11:6** also **Prov. 4:23; 11:27**

7. **Rejoice always in Hope.** Our greatest hope is living with our Lord forever. **Psalm 23:6** those who believe are sealed with the Holy Spirt that has been poured out into our hearts **Romans 5:5;** also **Rom.15:13: 2 Thess.5:16; Ps 119:162**

8. **Be patient in times of trouble**. When the word of God is planted deep within your heart, good things will follow, **Luke 8:15.** God is with us always **Matthew 28:20**

9. **Be steadfast in prayer.** Prayer is the lifeblood of communion with God as is the air we breathe. Pray often and always, **2 Thessalonians 5:16.** The Lord's prayer **Matthew 6:9-13; Psalm 23** the Lord is my shepherd.

10. **Distribute to the poor and the infirmed with hospitality.** Giving from the heart and having compassion for others with less is the hallmark of a Christian. A willingness to share not only money, but our home, abilities, talents and time.

11. **Bless those who curse you**. This is patience and forgiveness, along with praying that one day they will see the light in Jesus Christ. **(See Matthew 5:44)** Forgiveness of those who have hurt you, or wronged you releases you from the bitterness, resentment and anger in your own heart. It's good to forgive best to forget and move on with your life.

12. **Do not be wise in your own eyes.** Fear the Lord and depart from evil. **(Proverbs 3:7)** The lord searches the heart. **(Proverbs 21:2)** Be humble **(James 4:10; Prov. 3:34)** Be swift to hear slow to speak. **(James 1:19)**

13. **Repay no evil for evil**. The Son of God, Jesus Christ, sacrificed His life because of His love for us and said shortly before His death in **Luke 23:34** "Father, forgive them, for they do not know what they do." Let us always remember these words in our heart and follow this glorious act of grace.

14. **Live peacefully with all men.** One of God's desires is that we all live in peace and in harmony with our fellow man. **Isaiah 9:6-7** calls the coming of Christ Jesus "The Everlasting Father, Prince of Peace." At the birth of Christ in **Luke 2:14** "Glory to God in the highest, and on earth, peace, goodwill toward men! "Jesus himself said in **John 16:33** "In Me you shall have peace. In the world you will have tribulation; but be of good cheer, I have overcome the world.

Do, be, and live by these traits and the Lord will be with you in all that you do. Above all else do nothing without love and all in the name of our Lord and Savior Jesus Christ!!

CHAPTER 8

Relationships

————— ∞ —————

IF YOU ARE A LIVING, breathing human being you cannot help but be in relationships. There is nowhere that you can go that you are not in contact with other living human beings. God has fashioned and created us to live with others, so we are social creatures by nature. In **Genesis 1:28** "God blessed His creation of Man and Woman and told them to be fruitful and multiply and fill the earth."

According to the dictionary, we shall define a relationship as follows: The way in which people are connected and behave toward one another. Fellowship will also be included in our definition, in that it is a friendly association with people sharing like interests.

There are many different relationships that we have in our lives. We have intimate relationships personal relationships, close friend relationships, work relationships, interpersonal relationships, family relationships, social relationships, community relationships and church relationships to name several.

These are common characteristics that are shared with most of these relationships. Some, of course, are more important in maintaining long healthy relationships, but all in one degree or another are important.

The greatest relationship that one can have is with Jesus Christ our Lord and Savior. All other relationships can then flow out of the endless love He has for us and the love we in turn have for Him. When our heart is filled with this great love all other relationships in your life will flourish as a result. **1 John 1:19** "We love because He first loved us."

Here is a list of traits that are key to having healthy relationships with others:

1. **Self- love** - If you can't love yourself and the person you are, you will not have much to give in any relationship. This is not love in an egotistical or vain sense, but out of the love that comes from Christ. **Romans 9:39** "Nothing can separate us from the love of God."

2. **Trust** - Is key to any relationship. We must have complete confidence that we will always be there for one another in good times or bad. Do what you say you will do, be dependable and reliable. **Proverbs 3:5,6** "Trust in the Lord with all your heart and lean not on your own understanding; In all your ways acknowledge Him, and He will direct your path."

3. **Honesty**- Always speak the truth, relationships have no tolerance for lies and deceptions. Jesus said in **John 8:32** "Know the truth and the truth will set you free."

4. **Communication** – Must have a willingness to be open and share goals, dreams, joys, issues and concerns. Must be willing to talk things out. Listening is by far the key to

long lasting relationships. **Proverbs 8:34** "Blessed is the man who listens to Me."

5. **Acceptance** – Must accept the other person, faults and all, without the need to change or correct them. **Ephesians 1:6** "To the praise of the glory of His grace, by which he made us accepted in the Beloved."

6. **Respect** - Always treat others the way you want to be treated. Allow the other person privacy and space. Everyone needs time alone. For as Jesus said in **Matthew 7:12** "Whatever you want men to do to you, do also to them."

7. **Commitment** – Loyalty, dedication and willingness to do whatever it takes to make the relationship strong. **Proverbs 16:3** "Commit your works to the Lord and your thoughts will be established."

8. **Cooperation** – Always working together and sharing tasks, duties and responsibilities.

9. **Compromise** - A willingness to hear and understand the other points of view. Not always insisting just on your way of thinking and doing things.

10. **Connection** - Paying attention to the feelings, thoughts and interests of one another and be physically, emotionally, mentally and spiritually present with them.

11. **Appreciation** – Always remember the pleases and thank you's, and let people know you value them and their

contributions to the relationship. **1 Thessalonians 5:18** "In everything give thanks; for it is the will of God in Christ Jesus for you."

12. **Forgiveness** - We all make mistakes. Christ paid the ultimate sacrifice to forgive you, so forgiving others is critical to any relationship. Remember you are not condoning the behavior of the wrong done to you, just not allowing the anger, hurt, or disappointment to fester inside of you. **Ephesians 1:7** "In Him we have redemption through His blood, the forgiveness of sins according to the riches of His grace."

There will always be times in any of these relationships were disagreement and conflicts arise. Here are some helpful suggestions to help you through those times. **1.** Set a time when both of you can sit down and talk about it. **2.** Turn off all phones, TV's and all other distractions. **3.** Agree to listen to one another without the need to interrupt what the other is saying. **4.** Use "I" messages and speak to the behavior and not the person. Use the phrase "I feel, or I am"; then name or describe the behavior. What you are doing is taking ownership of your feelings or thoughts without the need to accuse or blame the other person. When you say "You make me feel" it immediately puts the other person on the defensive. **5.** The listening party can then respond with; "what I am hearing you say is this? is that right? This helps avoid misunderstanding and focuses on the behavior causing the problem, not the person.

Most all conflicts in relationships are the result of misunderstandings, making assumptions and the need to always be right. It would help us to reflect on this truth **Proverbs 21:2** "Every way of a man is right in his own eyes, but the Lord weighs the heart."

When we come to understand this, you can accept this truth as found in **Proverbs 23:19** "Hear my son and be wise; and guide your heart in the way."

When we spend time in prayer and in God's words of love, truth and grace we become better people on the inside resulting in improved relationships on the outside. God's greatest desire is for us to be in a relationship with Him. He wants to help us, strengthen us and fully embrace us with His never-ending love.

CHAPTER 9

We Reap What We Sow

MOST ALL OF US KNOW this title as it applies to gardening, farming and growing produce. Sow a crop, reap a harvest. The first step of planting, is that the soil must be properly tilled to form the right seedbed with weeds eliminated. The seed or plants need planted at just the right depth, not to deep, and not to shallow. The seed needs moisture and the proper amount of fertilizer to keep it healthy for growth.

The same is true in our lives as well. We must properly prepare our hearts to allow God's light and truth to be planted. We must pull up the weeds of anger, fear, worry, anxiety and despair and let God's love in. **Hosea 10: 12** "Sow for yourselves righteousness; Reap in mercy; Break up that fallow ground, for it is time to seek the Lord." We must then spend time in God's word through scripture, devotionals, and through prayer.

All throughout scripture and especially during Jesus' ministry we hear a great deal about being fruitful, bearing fruit, planting seeds and harvesting. This language was used to give people a better understanding of what was being said and what they should do to serve and obey God's commands and His ways. The same words are as true today as they were 2000 years ago.

The parable of the sower best describes where I was as a hypocrite for over 53 years. Pretending to be a Christian on the outside while living my own selfish ways on the inside. The desires of my heart were anything but God's ways. As Jesus said in Matthew **13:13** "Therefore I speak to them in parables, because seeing they do not see, and hearing they do not hear, nor do they understand."

That, my friends, is where I was most of my life, and it could be exactly where you are at with your life as well. How foolish and ignorant I was.

As Jesus says in **Matthew 13: 19-23** "When anyone hears the word of the Kingdom and does not understand it, the wicked one comes and snatches away what was sown in the heart. This is the one who received seed by the wayside. But he who received the seed on stony places, this is he who hears the word and immediately receives it with joy; yet he has not root in himself but endures only for a while. For when tribulation or persecutions arises because of the word, immediately he stumbles. He who received seed among the thorns is he who hears the word, and then the cares of the world and deceitfulness of riches chokes the word, he becomes unfruitful. But he who receives seed on the good ground is he who hears the word and understands it, who indeed bears fruit and produces, some a hundredfold, some sixty, some thirty. "

Is it possible like me, that you are struggling in life because you just can't accept God's word as truth? Is your heart just not in the right place to allow the Lord to plant His seeds of love, grace and truth?

What Jesus is telling us is that we will live with the results of our actions and need to pay attention to understand what is being said. Jesus' words are the source of our power that helps us make good decisions and gives us the thoughts to shape our hearts and minds.

Jesus said in **Matthew 7:24** "Whoever hears these sayings of Mine, and does them, I will liken him to a wise man who builds his house on the rock."

Galatians 6: 8,9 "For He who sows to the flesh will of the flesh reap corruption, but He who sows to the Spirit will of the Spirit reap everlasting life. And let us not grow weary while doing good, for in due season we shall reap if we do not lose heart."

Make no mistake about, should you continue to reject and rebel against God you will pay a price of condemnation." We will all be judged for our actions.

1 Corinthians 5:10 "For we must all appear before the judgement seat of Christ, that each one may receive the things done in the body, whether good or bad."

Jeremiah 17:5 Thus says the Lord "Cursed is the man who trusts in man and makes flesh his strength, whose heart departs from the Lord."

Jeremiah 17:9-10 "The heart is deceitful above all things and desperately wicked; who can know it? I, the Lord search the heart, I test the mind, even to give every man according to his ways, According to the fruit of his doings."

Proverbs 5:21,22 "For the ways of man are before the eyes of the Lord. And He ponders all his paths, his own iniquities entrap the wicked man, and he is caught in the cords of his sin."

There is a quote from Charles Reade and is known as the law of the harvest "Sow a thought-reap an action; Sow an action - reap a habit; Sow a habit - reap a character; Sow a character – reap a destiny."

James 3:17,18 "The wisdom that is from above is first pure, then peaceable, gentle, willing to yield, full of mercy and good fruits, without partiality and without hypocrisy. Now the fruit of righteousness is sown in peace by those who make peace."

Sowing God's words are at the heart of what Jesus commands all Christians to be doing, to draw more people into the loving Kingdom of God. Searching and seeking out lost souls is spreading God's words of truth and love to those in need and in despair. Serving the needs of the poor and elderly within our communities is always God's way of taking care of one another.

We all have choices on what we sow in our hearts and in our minds. Once the seeds of love, truth, goodness and peace are sown to others, we can and will reap a harvest for the Kingdom of God.

Sow Love, Sow Peace, Sow Hope, Sow Encouragement, Sow goodness, Sow Compassion, Sow Gentleness, Sow Support, Sow patience, Sow Kindness, Sow justice, Sow Righteousness, Sow Truth, Sow Loyalty and Commitment, Sow Joy and Happiness. Above all else, Sow love in your heart and do what is pleasing to God and in return Reap Everlasting Life.

Lord Make Me an Instrument of Your Peace Prayer
Lord, make me an instrument of your peace.
Where there is hatred, let me sow love;
Where there is injury, pardon;

Where there is doubt, faith;
Where there is despair, hope;
Where there is darkness, light;
Where there is sadness, joy;
O Divine Master, Grant that I may not so
much seek to be consoled as to console;
To be understood as to understand; To be
loved as to love. For it is in giving
That we receive; It is in pardoning that we are pardoned;
And it is in dying that we are born to eternal life.

CHAPTER 10

Saving Faith

———⚬⚬⚬———

THERE ARE MANY CHRISTIANS WHO say they are believers in Jesus Christ. Many believe that he does exist and is who He claims to be – the Son of God and that He is the savior of the world. Many also think that because they believe in God that their sins are forgiven and that their belief is enough to get them to everlasting life.

Is this simple belief in God enough? Is having belief just the same as having saving faith? The answer is No, it is not enough just to say you believe and we will look at the differences.

A Belief is an acceptance of assumed truth or that something or someone exits and is considered true. We use beliefs to help us understand the world we live in. I can have beliefs about things or people that do not affect my life whatsoever. I can believe that plastic is better than Styrofoam, but that fact alone does not impact how I live my life. I can believe football is better than basketball, but this too has no personal commitment on how I live my life, or a dependence on that fact. A belief is more of an intellectual exercise and is not from the heart.

Saving faith on the other hand shall be defined as having complete heart felt trust in Jesus Christ for forgiveness of sins and for eternal life with God. Belief most certainly is a vital element of faith but does not have the personal trust and dependence on Jesus for salvation and the guarantee of everlasting life.

Trust then is the critical link in saving faith that believing does not have. Saving faith is also a belief coming from the heart, mind and soul and involves how one lives their lives for and through Jesus Christ in the Spirit. When you are trusting in Christ, you are surrendering all of yourself, no matter what life circumstances you find yourself in; whether good or bad.

Jesus says in **John 3:16** "That whoever believes in Him should not perish but have eternal life." We can see that Jesus didn't just say believe Him, He says believe in Him meaning there is a union of coming into Him as a believer. This would also indicate that a personal trust of faith comes from the heart and is not just an intellectual exercise.

Saving faith is having a personal relationship with God and spending time in reading His words of truth. It is praying daily, giving thanks, asking for forgiveness, with a willingness to obey and follow His commands.

Jesus speaks to us in several places about "come to Me" such as in **John 6:37** "All that the Father gives to Me will come to Me, and the one who comes to Me, I will by no means cast out." Also, Jesus says in **John 7:37** "If anyone thirsts let him come to Me and drink."

In another verse, Jesus says in **Matthew 11:28-30** "Come to Me, all you who labor and are heavy laden, and I will give you rest. Take My yoke upon you and learn from Me, for I am gentle and lowly in heart, and you will find rest for your souls. For My yoke is easy and My burden is light."

These verses all say there is much more involvement and commitment from us with saving faith. There are essential elements that are needed for saving faith. **1.** Must have some knowledge of the Gospel and know about God. **2.** Must totally accept that the words spoken in all of scripture is true. **3.** Must trust completely and submit your life to Christ for salvation, the need to repent, and that Jesus is the only way to God.

It will be helpful to look at two verses which tie directly into what saving faith is and how the Holy Spirit comes alive within us. **John 1:12,13** "He gave the right to become children of God to those who believe in His name; who were born, not of blood nor of the will of the flesh, nor or the will of man, but of God."

Also, as Jesus said in **John 3:3-8** "Most assuredly, I say to you, unless one is born again, he cannot see the kingdom of God. Unless one is born of water and the Spirit, he cannot enter the kingdom of God. That which is born of the flesh is flesh, and that which is born of the Spirit is spirit. Do not marvel that I said to you, you must be born again. The wind blows where it wishes, and you hear the sound of it, but cannot tell where it comes from and where it goes. So is everyone who is born of the Spirit."

This of course, is where we get the term Re-born again Christians. Theologians call this regeneration and will be defined as follows: Regeneration is something that comes only from God in which He imparts new spiritual life within us. We play no part whatsoever in this action. It just happens to us.

As a non-believer for over 53 years, I will absolutely testify and bear witness to God Almighty that it does just happen. I spent 15 months reading my wife's devotional books shortly after her death 3 years ago, to cope with the pain of losing her. One day, 15 months later, I suddenly felt the presence of God within me, and by His grace, filled my heart with His love. Words just can't describe that moment, for I have never in my life been filled with such Joy, Peace and Calm. To this day I am in reverent awe over the power of the Holy Spirit that is working within me to write and share my faith with others.

Further scripture concerning regeneration and saving faith are included in **Ephesians 2: 5,8** "Even when we were dead in trespasses, made us alive together with Christ. For by grace you have been saved through faith and that not of yourselves; it is a gift of God." Also, **Ephesians 3:16,17** "That He would grant you, according to the riches of His glory, to be strengthened with might through His Spirit in the inner man, that Christ may dwell in your hearts through faith; that you be rooted and grounded in love."

Additional verses of the Holy Spirit working and dwelling in us, we can turn to **Galatians 2:20** "I have been crucified with Christ; it is no longer I who live, but Christ lives in me; and the life I now live in the flesh, I live by faith in the Son of God, who loved me an gave Himself for me." Also, **Romans 8:10** "And if Christ is in you, the body is dead because of sin, but the Spirit is life because of righteousness."

Some of you may be asking, "How will I know when the Holy Spirit is alive within me?" You will know immediately when God's grace fills your heart. The presence of the Holy Spirit will be felt inside of you as He pours the love of God into your heart. You will have a deep desire and a thirst to spend more time in His word. You will begin earnestly praying more and more. You will want to have more fellowship with other believers.

You will want to share your faith with others. You will become more obedient to Gods words of truth and live more in the spirit of Christ with a lesser desire to seek passions of the flesh. You will also look to ways on how to become a better servant of the Lord with a desire to serve others at church and in your community.

This is how it all happened with me and it may be different with others. I was a non-believer for many years and if you have been growing in your faith over a number of years, it sure could be much different. I will still say, you will know when you have been empowered with the Holy Spirit and He begins working within you. You will discover, a joy, a peace and a contentment unlike anything you have never experienced. Your life will change with a deep sense of worship, praise, gratitude and an eager willingness to serve one another in brotherly love and kindness.

Spiritual Growth

ONCE YOU BECOME A TRUE believer, you will want to seek more of the enlightenment and power of the Holy Spirit within you. **1 John 4:4** "Greater is He who is in you than he who is in the world." You will begin understanding what God's purpose and will for your life is and become more focused on His will and His ways and the need to give up your old selfish ways.

One way to find out where you are in with your spiritual growth is to pay attention to what you do and say to yourself when you first get up in the morning. How we start the day is a key to how the rest of your day will go. Do you stumble out of bed, hit the snooze 3 or 4 times, not wanting to get up or do you hit the ground running. We are all creatures of habit so whatever it is that you do, start taking notice of what you are saying or thinking to yourself.

Do your thoughts sound something like this: "I don't want to be up" I just want to go back to bed" "I am so tired, don't want to go to work" "Oh, if only I didn't have to work" etc.? Then, do you begin thinking about what all must be done for the day. Too much to do, no time to get it all done. It's like the day is shot before it has even started!!

I know these thoughts all to well and have had them with me most of my life. That is until now, since I have turned my life over to Christ and found a better way to get started for the day. It's just a mindset, a change on what I am saying to myself not only to start the day but throughout the day as well.

"Thank you, Father, for another day, help me and give me strength for today." "Help me focus today on your will and not mine." "Send out your light and your truth today, Father, and let them lead me." (see **Psalm 43:3)**

"Draw close to me today, Father, let me feel your presence." (see **James 4:8**) "Father, help keep my heart and mind focused on you today."

These are several ways to jumpstart your day. There are many verses of encouragement and inspiration throughout the old and new testament. I have included Inspirational verses at the end of the book for quick reference.

This has worked for me and helps break the bad habit of negative thinking and on into the personal and spiritual realm of God. Starting the day by thanking the Lord and asking for strength is a much better way. **Psalm 31:4,5** "Lead me and guide me, for You are my strength, into your hand I commit my spirit."

The work of the Holy Spirit is the active presence of God in this world. **Job 12:10** "He is the life source of all living creatures and the breath of all mankind." Also, in **Psalm 104:30** "You send forth Your Spirit, they are created." We then see how without the Spirit what would happen to man in **Job 34:14-15** "If He should gather to Himself His Spirit and His breath, all flesh would perish together, and man would return to dust."

He is active in regeneration and saving faith as discussed in the last chapter. The Holy Spirit descended on Jesus' baptism in **Matthew 3:16**. The Holy Spirit is part of baptism for all confessing their belief and repentance of sin. **Acts 2:38** "Repent and let everyone be baptized in the name of Jesus Christ for the remission of sins; and you shall receive the Holy Spirit." In preaching, reading and teaching of Scripture, the Holy Spirit speaks to people's hearts.

In prayer the Holy Spirit intercedes for us and helps us in our weakness as found in **Romans 8: 26** "The Spirit helps us in our weaknesses, for we do not know what we should pray for as we ought, but the Spirit himself makes intercession for us with groaning which cannot be uttered." We also gain access to one Spirit to the Father in **Ephesians 2:18** "For through Him we both have access by one Spirit to the Father."

The most important decision you can make that will bring about real meaning and purpose in your life is to submit to God and get to know Him and His words of truth.

For as Jesus said in **John 8:32** "Know the truth and the truth will set you free." Jesus again said in **John 6:63** "It is the Spirit who gives life, the flesh profits nothing. The words that I speak to you are spirit and they are life."

In **Galatians 5,** the Apostle Paul compares what living in the flesh and living in the spirit entails. Paul says that if we walk in the Spirit you will not fulfill the lust of the flesh. **Gal. 5:16**.

He further states that the flesh lusts against the Spirit and the Spirit against the flesh. These are contrary to one another and do not allow you to do the things you desire. **v 17** If you are led by the Spirit you are not under the law. **v18** Paul lists the works of the flesh (sins) which are adultery, fornication, uncleanness, lewdness, idolatry, hatred, contentions, jealousies, outbursts of wrath, selfish ambitions, dissensions, heresies, envy, murders, drunkenness and revelries. **v19,20**. He then issues a warning that those who practice such things will not inherit the Kingdom of God.

Paul then lists the fruit of the Spirit which is love, joy, peace, patience, kindness goodness, faithfulness, gentleness, and self-control against such there is no law. **v22,23**

Paul finishes up with, those who are Christ's have crucified the flesh with its passions and desires. **v24.** and that if we live in the Spirit, let us also walk in the Spirit. **v25**

Jesus said in **John 4:24** "God is Spirit, and those who worship Him must worship in spirit and in truth." We clearly see that giving up old ways of living and walking in the Spirit is the only way free ourselves from the grip of the God of this world, Satan. Living through Christ and with Christ and For Christ is all done through the Holy Spirit who dwells within true believes.

Getting to know God requires a commitment and these four things:

1. An open bible

2. An open mind and heart

3. A willingness to learn and grow

4. Time set aside on a daily basis for reading and praying.

There are countless devotional guides available which are very helpful, or you can follow this simple guide.

1. Your commitment of an open heart and mind

2. A willingness to learn and grow daily – not whenever you feel like it or can find the time to do it, but daily.

3. A quiet place to clear your mind, no interruptions. **Psalm 46:10** "Be still and know that I am God."

4. Have a notebook handy along with a highlighter to write down or mark passages that speak to you.

5. Pray to the Lord and ask him for understanding on the words and passages you read.

6. Start with any of the four Gospels: Matthew, Mark, Luke or John, for these are the teachings of Jesus. From there you will find many verses in the fourteen epistles written by the Apostle Paul, Psalms, Proverbs, Isaiah, and Jeremiah.

7. Pray again and thank the Lord for what you have read.

There is no set secret formula that works for everybody: What matters most is that you start allowing God into

your life and into your heart daily, not just weekly or when you feel like it.

Stick with this plan and you will discover, as I have the power and the words of wisdom, He speaks to you. You will begin feeling more and more of His presence and His desire to have you close to Him. Give the Lord time each day through reading and praying and your life will forever be changed to one of peace, joy and hope for a better future. **Psalm 37:4.5** "Delight yourself daily in the Lord and He shall give you the desires of your heart. Commit your ways to the Lord and trust in Him."

CHAPTER 12

Treasures of the Heart

TRUE HAPPINESS IS NOT A when, or a where; it is a now. It's not what you have or what you do or even the people closest to you that bring about true happiness. Happiness is quite simply who you are! And who are you? You are a child of God; created, fashioned and molded by His loving hands and in the likeness of His image. **Genesis 1:27** You are loved beyond comprehension by God, and He cares deeply about you and wants nothing but the best for you. **Romans 8:39 and Jeremiah 29:11**

You cannot find happiness in a **When I** − make or have more money, get a better job, find a mate, own a bigger house, have designer clothes, jewelry, etc. This is because those are things outside of yourself. They are external things. Chasing after material things, possessions, relying on others for your happiness, and wanting things is truly a lie that you have accepted as true.

Happiness and the true meaning of life are found in your heart. And your heart is the innermost part of your being. It is the center of all your thoughts, emotions, intuition, feelings and your deepest desires. It is the wellspring that motivates and springs you into action and is where the issues of life are truly found. **Proverbs**

4:23 "Keep your heart with all diligence, for out of it spring the issues of life."

God's greatest desire is to plant the seeds of love, truth and grace into your heart and to develop a loving personal relationship with you. With God's word firmly established in your heart, you will take on a whole new level of Joy, Peace and contentment unlike anything you have ever known.

God's peace and joy are hard to fully comprehend and is beyond human understanding. **Colossians 4:14,15** "Above all things, put on love, which is the bond of perfection, and let the peace of God rule in your hearts." **Philippians 4:7** "The peace of God, which surpasses all understanding, will guard your hearts and minds through Jesus Christ."

The Bible has over 900 verses with the word heart or hearts. They reflect how important and essential the heart is when truly believing in our Lord and Savior Jesus Christ. Many so-called Christians can know about God and say they believe in Him, but don't truly have Him in their heart.

Several words of truth speak to that and of course the greatest of these was spoken by Jesus in **Matthew 22:37-39** "You shall love the Lord your God with all your heart, with all your soul and with all your mind. This is the greatest commandment. And the second is like it; You shall love your neighbor as yourself." Also found in **Romans 10:8,9,10** "The word is near you, in your mouth and in your heart. (that is the word of faith which we preach.)" That if you confess with your mouth the Lord Jesus and believe in your heart that God has raised Him from the dead, you will be saved.

"For with the heart one believes unto righteousness, and with the mouth confession is made unto salvation."

When we spend time in the word of God as found in scripture, we come to understand how His words of truth, wisdom and love speak to us in our heart. Without opening our hearts and minds to His words, we can never get to know God much less truly believe in Him.

All one needs to do is commit time daily in reading and praying and if you keep at it, you will discover as I have, the incredible wisdom, knowledge and love necessary to fulfill all of life's greatest treasures.

We also learn by study and reading His word, that the heart is at the root of all evil and the perverse ways that people will take in living their lives. We are either for God or we are against God, there is no middle ground.

For as Jesus said in **Matthew 12:30** "He who is not with Me is against Me, and he who does not gather with Me scatters abroad." We also know that what defiles a man comes out of his heart as Jesus said in **Matthew 15:18,19** "Those things which proceed out of the mouth come from the heart, and they defile a man. For out of the heart proceed evil thoughts, murders, adulteries, fornicators, thefts, false witnesses and blasphemies."

In James 3:14-16 "If you have bitter envy and self-seeking in your hearts, do not boast and lie against the truth. This wisdom does not descend from above, but is earthly, sensual, demonic. For where envy and self-seeking exist, confusion and every evil thing is there."

For 53 years I lived my life according to what the God of this world (Satan) had to offer and I pursued and chased after materials possessions and the pleasures of it. All those years of struggling without God in my life have all melted away and disappeared. I have some moments of doubts and worry, but it doesn't stay with me long, for I am learning to completely trust that God is always there.

He wants you to take your burdens, your worries, your fears and anger and help strengthen you and help you get through them. **1 Peter 5:7** "Cast all your cares upon Him, for He cares for you."

Also, in **Isaiah 41:10,11** "Fear not for I am with you; Be not dismayed, for I am your God, I will strengthen you, I will help you, I will uphold you in My righteous right hand."

We learn as we read and study, that God tests the hearts and minds in our lives, as found in **Jeremiah 17:9,10** "The heart is deceitful above all things, and desperately wicked; Who can know it? I, the Lord, search the heart, I test the mind, even to give every man according to his ways, according to the fruit of his doings." Also found in **Jeremiah 17:5** "Cursed is the man who trusts in man, and makes flesh his strength, whose heart departs from the Lord."

As discussed earlier in Chapter 10, trust is the key to saving faith and in coming into repentance and in regeneration thereby receiving the gift of the Holy Spirit. Fully and completely trusting in God requires that 100% of your entire being (heart, mind and soul) is committed to His will and to His ways.

When your heart is right and aligned with the Lord, your whole life will change and you will take great joy and delight in all that you say, do and think. **Psalm 37:3,4** "Trust in the Lord and do good; dwell in the land and feed on His faithfulness.

Delight yourself also in the Lord, and He shall give you the desires of your heart." You will also want to carry out Gods will in your life and be a faithful servant. **Psalm 40:8** "I delight to do Your will, O my God, and Your law is within my heart."

When we turn our hearts away from God and reject Him, He will harden our hearts, blind us to the truth, make us unable to hear or understand His word. **Isaiah 6:9,10** and the Lord said "tell these people: keep on hearing, but do not understand; Keep on seeing, but do not perceive. Make the heart of this people dull, and their ears heavy, and shut their eyes; Lest they see with their eyes, and hear with their ears, and understand with their heart, and return and be healed."

When we do not acknowledge His words of truth nor abide by His ways, He will give us the desires of our heart. We see this in **Romans 1:24**, "Therefore God also gave them up to uncleanness, in the lusts of their hearts, to dishonor their bodies among themselves, who exchanged the truth of God for the lie, and worshiped and served the creature rather than the Creator, who is blessed forever."

Placing anything above God is idolatry and is not exalting or glorifying Him as He so richly and rightfully deserves. For as Jesus said when tempted by Satan in **Matthew 4:10** "You shall worship the Lord your God, and Him only you shall serve."

And again, when tempted Jesus said in Matt **4:4** "Man shall not live by bread alone, but every word that proceeds from the mouth of God."

If you are having problems, struggles, concerns and issues in your life right now, turn your life over to Christ who is the only one who can strengthen and help you. Seek out the Lord with all your heart and He will give you the courage and strength to overcome whatever challenges you face. As it is said in **James 4:8** "Draw close to the Lord and He will draw close to You"

CHAPTER 13

Letting God Into your Life

AS WE HAVE DISCUSSED THROUGHOUT the book, we all have an innate desire to live according to the pleasures of the world. We seek to satisfy our lives with careers, money, power, status and material possessions. We covet what others have and all desires of the heart are for our own self-satisfaction and our own selfish ways of living. Our own self-serving interests, pride and control are what keep us blinded by the truth.

We do all this with little thought or regard for God the Father, who gives us all things, who sustains us, and who provides for us daily. Why do you suppose we do this? Why do we continue to rebel and live our lives without God in it? What makes it so hard to realize that God is in control of everything here on earth and in the heavens above?

If you are like me, for many years, we do all these things because we want to be in control of everything in our lives. We don't want someone telling us how to live our lives. It's our choice, it's our decision on how best to live. We just get so busy pursuing goals and trying to be successful that there just doesn't seem to be enough time left over for God.

As stated in the last chapter God does all of this to test us, to see if we will turn the desires of our heart to Him. (see **Jeremiah 17:9,10.**) What happens with most of us is that we suppress the truth, and then God further hardens our hearts to give us what we desire the most which is worldly pleasures. (see **Romans 1:24.)**

For many of us the suppressing of truth and believing in the lies, leaves us with feelings of restlessness and a sense of longing or lost for real meaning and purpose in our life. We don't really ever feel fulfilled or completely satisfied. As a result, to ease this restlessness, we fill the void with excessive drinking, drugs, gambling, sex, work 70 hours a week, shop excessively, buy things we don't need.

As the Lord said in **Isaiah 55:2,3** "Why do you spend money for what is not bread, and your wages for what does not satisfy? Listen carefully to Me, and eat what is good, and let your soul delight itself in abundance. Incline your ear, and come to Me. Hear, and your soul shall live."

The bread in this verse is referring to the bread of deceit as found in **Proverbs 20:17** "Bread gained by deceit is sweet to a man, but afterward his mouth will be filled with gravel." Rather than the good bread as spoken by Jesus in **John 6:35** "I am the bread of life, he who comes to Me shall never hunger, and he who believes in Me, shall never thirst." The bread also refers to the nourishment of the soul as spoken in **Luke 4:4** "Man shall not live on bread alone, but every word of God."

Now we all know that we are sinners. **Romans 3:23** "For all have sinned and fall short of the glory of God." And again, in **Romans 3:12** "There is none who does good, no, not one." So how is it that

God still allows us sinners, to go about living our lives in total disobedience and living anyway we please?

The answer to that question can best be described in **Romans 5:20,21** "Where sin abounded, grace abounded more, so that as sin reigned in death, even so grace might reign through righteousness to eternal life through Jesus Christ our Lord."

It is through God's divine love, mercy and grace which allows sinners a delay in their punishment for death and eternal damnation. The reasons for this delay in judgement can be found in **Ezekiel 33:11** "As I live, says the Lord God, I have no pleasure in the death of the wicked, but that the wicked turn from his ways and live. Turn, turn from your evil ways! For why should you die."

God desires that all his people be saved by repentance and the knowledge of truth as written in **1 Timothy 2:4** "God our Savior, desires all men to be saved and to come to the knowledge of the truth."

The Lord continues to encourage and give people time to seek Him out and to acknowledge His existence and develop a personal relationship with Him. So how does one receive the gift of grace which only comes from God? Grace as we know it, cannot be earned by us. We are saved by faith and it must be a sincere faith of the heart.

It is not lip service or just an intellectual exercise of a token belief. It is true genuine faith and a deep love of Jesus Christ who is the only one who can save us from condemnation.

There are only two ways to become a true believer and that requires a commitment on your part. It will require you to begin reading scripture and allow God to speak to you through His word. A devotional guide can also be used. You cannot just read intellectually but must search and understand what the Lord is saying to you through your heart.

It will take time, so patience is critical. You must also be diligent and do this daily, not whenever you feel like it. **Proverbs 4:23** "Keep your heart with all diligence for out of it spring the issues of life."

Attending church services can also be very beneficial as well as joining a bible study. Being around other believers will certainly help in your growth process. I will repeat what I said at the very beginning of the book when Christ enter my life and filled my heart with the Holy Spirit. Words cannot describe the joy, the peace and the calm that filled my soul. It was exhilarating, breathtaking and so inspiring with feelings that I have never before experienced.

Daily prayer is the second way to become a true believer. **Matthew 26:41** "Pray always for the flesh is weak but our Spirit is strong and willing." Ask the Lord to fill your heart with His love, truth and mercy. Asking for forgiveness is part of the process of getting to know God. Thanking the Lord always for the countless blessings He sends out to you on a daily basis is a must. **Ephesians 5:20** "Give thanks always for all things to God the Father in the name of our Lord Jesus Christ."

Seeking His guidance, instruction and teaching of His ways and for His will. **Isaiah 48:17** "I am the Lord who teaches you and leads you by the way you should go." Asking Him to send out His light to lead you down the path of righteousness. **Psalm 43:3** "O Lord, send out Your light and Your truth and let them lead me."

Praying for knowledge, wisdom and understanding are also requests you can make to the Lord. **James 1:5** "If any of you lacks wisdom, let him ask of God, who gives to all liberally and without reproach, and it will be given to you." As Jesus said in **Matthew 7:7,8** "Ask, and it will be given to you; seek, and you will find; knock, and it will be opened to you. For everyone who asks receives, and he who seeks finds, and to him who knocks it will be opened."

Isaiah 55:6 "Seek the Lord while He may be found, call upon Him while He is near." **Psalm 34:4** "I sought the Lord, and He heard me, and delivered me from all fears." God will listen and when he knows your heart is right and ready to hear His words of truth He will respond. You must remember He may not respond right away.

If you remain persistent with your reading and with your prayers, one day God's grace will fill your heart with love by the power of the Holy Spirit who will be given to you.

I will assure you that the joy, peace and calm on that day will be unlike anything you have ever known. You will be, as I was, in reverent awe over this life changing transformation and your whole life will take on a much deeper level of meaning and purpose!!

God deeply loves and cares for you and His greatest desire is to for you to seek Him out and develop a personal relationship with Him. **Allowing Christ Jesus into you heart and completely trusting in Him is by far the most important decision you will ever make.** He will empower you, strengthen you and help you resolve any burdens or problems you are having. His words of truth, wisdom and promises of a better future will inspire you and will lead you to a whole new level of Happiness, Peace and Joy! **Jeremiah 29: 11-13** "For I know the plans I have for you declares the Lord, plans to prosper you and not to harm you, plans to give you hope and a future. Then you will call on Me and come and pray to Me, and I will listen to you. You will seek Me and find Me when you seek Me with all your heart."

Proverbs 3: 5,6 "Trust in the Lord with all your heart and lean not on your own understanding; In all your ways acknowledge Him, and He will direct your paths."

Philippians 4:13 "I can do all things through Christ who strengthens me."

CHAPTER 14

Hope

It is my hope that while reading this book you have gained a better understanding of the divine love that God has for you and that He wants only the best for you in your life. His goodness, faithfulness, mercy, grace and truth can lead you into a closer relationship with Him.

By spending time in His word and in praying more often, you will come to know God, not just know about Him. By reaching out to Him with a sincere heart, you will find a peace, joy and calm unlike anything you can imagine.

For many people, hope is found only by relying on themselves and trying to live their lives without any real need or help from God. Most of the time hope is an optimistic feeling that things will all work out well.

We hope that we get the job we have applied for. We hope that our children will make good decisions. We hope that the weather will cooperate for an outing. We hope we get the scholarship we applied for. We hope that a surgery or operation turns out well. We hope that we find something that we lost. We hope that we make the team. These are several of the ways that we hope and use hope throughout our lives.

The definition of hope in the dictionary is; a desire accompanied by expectation of or belief in fulfillment. Expect with confidence that something is doing well.

What happens when the hope of fulfillment and well-being don't turn out well? When someone is going through a divorce, a job loss, or the death of a loved one. The disappointment and anger when trying to find a new job isn't working out.

The fear and doubts when the sudden, dramatic change of living alone after years in a marriage and now having to rely on just one income. The impact that it has when children are involved and the guilt that overwhelms you for the breakup of a marriage.

The heartache of a loved one's death and the loneliness and emptiness without them. The reality of these events and life changes, can leave a person with little hope and even despair.

As the anger, disappointment, guilt, fears, doubts and uncertainties take hold, it can lead a person into depression and feelings of failure. As many of you will find out, relying on family and friends is not enough to get you through these life changing events. Professional counseling is helpful but even that is not a sure-fire way to get past the hurt, the pain and the fears one still can be left with.

There is a much better way of dealing with these issues and struggles in your life right now and His name is Jesus Christ. His comfort, His strength and His love for you will without a doubt help you regain a hope, a peace, a joy and a calm that will change your life forever.

Hope in the bible shall be defined as; a complete trust and confident expectation of what God has promised with His strength in faithfulness and endless love.

The essence of Christianity, salvation, and eternal life is Faith, Hope and Love as scripture says in **1 Corinthians 13:13** "So now faith, hope, and love abide, these three; but the greatest of these is love." Also, in **1 Corinthians 13:7,8** "Love bears all things, believes all things, hopes all things, endures all things. Love never ends." ESV.

When we talk about the hope found in our Lord and Savior Jesus Christ, we begin to understand that complete trust and faith in Him, can and will help you through whatever life circumstances and struggles come your way. He will comfort you, He will heal you and give you hope for a better life and a better way of living.

A good example of this is found in **Jeremiah 29:11-13** "For I know the plans I have for you, declares the Lord, plans to prosper you and not to harm you, plans to give you hope and a future. Then you will call on Me and come and pray to Me, and I will listen to You. You will seek Me and find Me when you seek Me with all your heart." NIV

As you begin to rely, trust, and depend on the Lord for everything in our life you will find a confidence and assurance that He is always there to help you. He will guide you, strengthen you and comfort you, through anything life throws at you. **Romans 5:5** "Now hope does not disappoint, because the love of God has been poured out into our hearts by the Holy Spirit who was given to us."

We see other verses of hope as found in **Psalm 31:24** "Be of good courage, and He shall strengthen your heart, all you who hope in the Lord." **Psalm 33:18,20,21,22** "Behold the eye of the Lord are on those who fear Him, on those who hope in His mercy. Our soul waits for the Lord; He is our help and our shield, for our heart shall rejoice in Him, because we have trusted in His holy name. Let your mercy, O Lord, be upon us, just as we hope in You."

Remember the fear of the Lord is a reverent awe and deep respect for who He is and to hate evil as He does.

As true believers, we eagerly await our adoption as Sons and Daughters as the promise made by God during salvation and the redemption of our bodies for, we were saved in this hope. **Romans 8 :24,25** "For we were saved in this hope, but hope that is seen is not hope; for why does one still hope for what he sees? But if we hope for what we do not see, we eagerly wait for it with perseverance."

The prophet Jeremiah in Lamentations is describing the funeral of a city around 586 BC. A once proud Jerusalem now reduced to rubble by the invading Babylonian empire. All hope is lost but then Jeremiah remembers that God has never failed Him in the past and has promised to remain faithful in the future.

Lamentations 3:21-26 "This I recall to my mind; Therefore, I have hope. Through the Lord's mercies we are not consumed, because His compassions fail not. They are new every morning; Great is Your faithfulness. The Lord is my portion, says my soul, therefore I hope in Him! The Lord is good to those who wait for Him, to the soul who seeks Him, it is good that one should hope and wait quietly for the salvation of the Lord."

Hope is something that requires patience and perseverance, and God delivers on His promises. Our time frames are far different than the Lord's. We tend to want things to happen now and immediately, but God knows all, sees all and knows when the time is right and what is best for us at any given moment and on His time frame not ours. We can rest assured that He will respond and deliver, what He deems to be the right path and direct us accordingly.

We, through hope in His faithfulness, mercies and love need to exercise patience. Patience by far is an area most of us completely lack. Traffic jams, doctors' offices, grocery store lines, waiting for anything is a major challenge for most of us, myself included. We expect our needs to be met right away, can't possibly wait to satisfy our desires.

We just can't wait another second to get what we think we can't live without. Must have this or that without delay, it's our nature to get that instant relief.

A good definition for patience is the ability to accept or tolerate delays, problems, or struggles without becoming annoyed or anxious.

Let me leave this chapter with these four verses to meditate on and fill your heart.

Romans 15:4 "For whatever things were written before were written for our learning, that we through the patience and comfort of the Scriptures might have hope."

Romans 15:13 "Now may the God of hope fill you with all joy and peace in believing, that you may abound in hope by the power of the Holy Spirit."

Galatians 5:5 "For we through the Spirit eagerly wait for the hope of righteousness by faith."

Hebrew 10:23 "Let us hold fast the confession of our hope without wavering, for He who promised is faithful."

I WISH TO THANK EACH and everyone of you for reading this book and allowing me to share my faith with you. I sincerely hope and pray that you will spend more time in prayer and reading God's words of truth, wisdom and the divine love He has for you.

Jesus Christ wants only the best for you and desires to have an intimate lasting relationship with you, now, and on into His greatest promise of everlasting life. Start today and make the most important decision of your life in getting to know God, not just know about Him.

Discover as I have, that when you allow Him into your heart and soul, you will experience the greatest joy, peace and calm unlike anything you have ever known. Through placing your trust in Him, you will ease many of the heavy burdens you carry and experience with everyday living.

With God in your life, you will see things in a much different way and understand how we all are in need of the Gospel and His encouraging words of love, truth, peace, comfort, hope and joy. Once His words are deeply embedded in your heart, you will gain, not only the true meaning of love and truth, but will begin understanding what the true treasures of life most certainly are.

I would love to hear from you and would deeply appreciate a review on Amazon with your feedback. You can send me an email directly at tstuckey@hotmail.com or go to my website at https://ted-stuckey2.com

May God's Love and Peace fill your heart each and every day !!

—಄಄—

LET THIS BE A QUICK reference to verses that can and will inspire you throughout the day or at the end of the day to help you relax and let God's words speak to you. Keep at this daily and you will find yourself in a more peaceful and relaxed state.

Psalm 94:19 "In the multitudes of my anxieties within me, your comforts delight my Soul."

Mark 9:23 "All things are possible to those who believe."

Psalm 25:4 "Show me your ways O Lord; teach me your paths, lead me in truth and teach me, for you are the God of my salvation."

Isaiah 41:10 "Fear not, for I am with you; Be not dismayed, for I am your God. I will strengthen you, I will help you, I will uphold you with My righteous right hand."

John 14:27 "Let not your heart be troubled, nor be afraid."

1 Corinthians 13:7 "Love bears all things, believes all things, hopes all things, endures all things. Love never fails."

Psalm 46:1 "God is my refuge and my strength."

Proverbs 30:5 "Every word of God is pure; He is a shield to those who put their trust in Him."

2 Samuel 22:33 "God is my strength and power, and He makes my way perfect."

Psalm 43:3 "Oh Lord, send out your light and truth and let them lead me."

Hebrew 13:20 "The God of peace gives you everything you need to do His will."

1 Chronicles 28:9 "For the Lord searches every heart and understands every desire and every thought."

Luke 4:4 "Man shall not live on bread alone, but by every word of God."

Psalm 35:17 "The righteous cry out and the Lord hears and delivers them out of their troubles."

John 6:63 "The Spirit gives life, the flesh profits nothing."

1 John 4:16 "He who abides in love abides in God and God in him."

Psalm 28:7 "The Lord is my strength and my shield, my heart trusted in Him and I am helped."

Psalm 31:24 "Be of good courage and He will strengthen your heart, all you who hope in the Lord."

1 John 3:20 "God is greater than our heart and knows all things.""

Psalm 62:8 "Trust in Him at all times, pour out your heart before Him; God is a refuge for us.

1 John 4:4 "He who is in you is greater than he who lives in this world."

Psalm 16:11 "You will show me the path of life, in your presence is fullness of joy; At your right hand are pleasures forevermore."

Philippians 4:6 "Be anxious for nothing but everything in prayer and supplication, with thanksgiving, let your requests be made known to God."

Philippians 4:7 "The peace of God, which surpasses all understanding, will guard your hearts and minds through Jesus Christ."

Philippians 4:13 "I can do all things through Christ who strengthens me."

Philippians 2:13 "For it is God who works in you, both to will and to do for His good pleasure."

Jeremiah 29:11 "For I know the plans I have for you, plans to prosper you and not to harm you, plans to give you hope and a future." NIV

Colossians 3:23 "Whatever you do, do it heartily, as to the Lord and not to men."

Colossians 3:14,15 "Above all things put on love, which is the bond of perfection, and let the peace of God rule in your hearts."

John 8:12 "I am the light of the world; He who follows Me shall not walk in darkness but have the light of life."

2 Timothy 1:7 "For God has not given us a Spirit of fear, but of power and of love and of a sound mind."

Hebrews 11:6 "Without faith it is impossible to please Him, for he who comes to God must believe that He is, and that He is a rewarder of those who diligently seek Him."

James 4:8 "Draw near to God and He will draw near to you, cleanse your hands, you sinners; and purify your hearts, you double minded."

1 Peter 5:6 "Humble yourselves under the mighty hand of the God that He may exalt you in due time, casting all your care upon Him, for He cares for you."

1 John 2:5 "Whoever keeps His word, truly the love of God is perfected in him, by this we know that we are in Him."

1 John 4:16 "We have known and believed the love that God has for us. God is love, and he who abides in love abides in God, and God in him."

Romans 1:16 "For I am not ashamed of the Gospel of Christ, for it is the power of God to salvation for everyone who believes."

Romans 6:14 "For sin shall not have dominion over you, for you are not under law but under grace."

Romans 8:1 "I thank God -through Jesus Christ our Lord! So then with the mind I myself serve the law of God, but with the flesh the law of sin."

Romans 8:28 "We know that all things work together for good to those who love God, to those who are called according to His purpose."

Romans 11:16 "If the first fruit is holy, the lump is also holy; and it the root is holy, so are the branches."

Romans 15:13 "Now may the God of hope fill you with all joy and peace in believing, that you may abound in hope by the power of the Holy Spirit."

1 Corinthians 1:30 "Of Him you are in Christ Jesus, who became for us wisdom from God, and righteousness and sanctification and redemption.

1 Corinthians 2:5 "That your faith should not be in the wisdom of men but in the power of God."

1 Corinthians 8:6 "There is one God the Father, of whom are all things, and we for Him; and one Lord Jesus Christ, through whom are all things, and through whom we live.

2 Corinthians 5:7 "For we walk by faith, not by sight."

2 Corinthians 12:9,10 Jesus said to the Apostle Paul "My grace is sufficient for you, for my strength is made perfect in weakness" therefore Paul said "I take pleasure in distress and tribulation for Christ's sake. "For when I am weak, then I am strong."

2 Corinthians 13:8 "For we can do nothing against the truth, but for the truth, for we are glad when we are weak, and you are strong."

Galatians 5:25" If we live in the Spirit, let us also walk in the Spirit."

Galatians 2:20 "For I have been crucified with Christ; It is no longer I who live, but Christ lives in me; and the life I live in the flesh, I live by faith in the Son of God, who loved me and gave Himself for me."

Galatians 6:9 "And let us not grow weary while doing good, for in due season we shall reap, if we do not lose heart.

2 Samuel 22:31 "As for God, His way is perfect; the word of the Lord is proven; He is a shield to all who trust in Him."

1 Samuel 16:7 "For the Lord does not see as man sees; for man looks at the outward appearance, but the Lord looks at the heart."

Job 12:11 "In the hand of God is the life of every living thing and the breath of all mankind." ESV

Ephesians 2:8 "For by grace you have been saved through faith, and that not of yourselves; it is the gift of God."

Ephesians 6:10 "Be strong in the Lord and in the power of His might."

Ephesians 1:19 "What is the exceeding greatness of His power toward us who believe, according to the working of His mighty power."

Isaiah 48:17 "I am the Lord your God, who teaches you to profit, who leads you by the way you should go."

Psalm 37:8 "Cease from anger, and do not fret, it only causes harm."

Psalm 46:11 "Be still and know that I am God."

Psalm 119:105 "Your word is a lamp to my feet, and a light to my path."

Ecclesiastes 1:9 "That which has been is what will be, that which is done is what will be done there is nothing new under the sun."

Ecclesiastes 3:1 "To everything there is a season, A time for every purpose under heaven.

John 6:35 "I am the bread of life, he who comes to Me shall never hunger, and he who believes in Me shall never thirst."

John 8:12 "I am the light of the world. He who follows Me shall not walk in darkness but have the light of life."

John 10:7 "I am the door of the sheep. If anyone enters by Me, He will be saved."

John 10:11 "I am the good shepherd; the good shepherd gives His life for the sheep."

John 11:25 "I am the resurrection and the life, he who believes in Me, though they may die, shall live, and he who lives and believes in Me shall never die."

John 14:6 "I am the way, the truth and the life, no one comes to the Father except through Me."

John 15:5 "I am the vine and you are the branches. He who abides in Me and I in him, bears much fruit, for without Me you can do nothing."

A P P E N D I X

———∞———

ADDITIONAL LOVE VERSES FROM CHAPTER 4

Matthew 5:44 Jesus said, "Love your enemies, bless those who curse you, do good to those who hate you, and pray for those who spitefully use you and persecute you."

John 14:15-17 Jesus said "If you love Me, keep My commandments. And I will pray the Father, and He will give you another Helper, that He may abide with you forever. The Spirit of truth, whom the world cannot receive, because it neither sees Him nor knows Him, for He dwells with you and will be with in you."

John 14:21 Jesus said, "He who loves Me will be loved by My Father, and I will love him and manifest Myself to him."

John 14:28 Jesus said "If you loved Me, you would rejoice because I said I am going to the Father, for My Father is greater than I."

John 15:12 Jesus said, "This is My commandment, that you love one another as I have loved you."

John 15:13 Jesus said, "Greater love has no one than this, than to lay down one's life for his friends."

John 17:26 Jesus said, "And I have declared to them Your name, and will declare it, that the love with which You loved Me may be in them, and I in them."

Roman 5:5 "Now hope does not disappoint, because the love of God has been poured out in our hearts, by the Holy Spirit who was given to us."

Romans 5:8 "But God demonstrates His own love toward us, in that while we were still sinners, Christ died for us."

Romans 8:28 "We know that all things work together for good to those who love God, to whose who are called according to His purpose."

Romans 8:39 "Nothing can separate us from the love of God which is in Christ Jesus our Lord."

1 Corinthians 13: 1-13 This is the longest description of love in all the Bible, written beautifully by the Apostle Paul

1 Corinthians 14:1 "Pursue love, and desire spiritual gifts."

2 Corinthians 13:11 "Be of good comfort, be of one mind, live in peace and the God of love and peace will be with you."

Galatians 5:6 "For in Christ Jesus neither circumcision nor uncircumcision avails anything, but faith working through love."

Galatians 5:20 "The fruit of the Spirit is love, joy, peace, patience, kindness, goodness, faithfulness, gentleness, self-control. Against such there is no law."

Ephesians 3:17 "That Christ may dwell in your hearts through faith; that you being rooted and grounded in love."

Ephesians 5:1 "Therefore be imitators of God as dear children, and walk in love, as Christ also has loved us and given Himself for us, an offering and a sacrifice to God for a sweet-smelling aroma."

2 Thessalonians 2:16,17 "Now may our Lord Jesus Christ Himself, and our God and Father, who has loved us and given us everlasting consolation and good hope by grace, comfort your hearts and establish you in every good word and work."

1 Timothy 1:5 "Now the purpose of the commandment is love from a pure heart, from a good conscience, and from sincere faith."

1 Timothy 1:14 "And the grace of our Lord was exceedingly abundant, with faith and love which are in Christ Jesus."

2 Timothy 1:7 "For God has not given us a spirit of fear, but of power and of love and of a sound mind."

2 Timothy 2:22 "Flee also youthful lusts; but pursue righteousness, faith, love, peace with those who call on the Lord out of a pure heart."

1 John 2:5 "Whoever keeps His word, truly the love of God is perfected in him. By this we know that we are in Him."

1 John 4:7,8 "Let us love one another, for love is of God; and everyone who loves if born of God and knows God. He who does not love does not know God, for God is love.

1 John 4:11 "If God so loved us, we also ought to love one another."

1 John 4:16 "And we have known and believed the love that God has for us. God is love, and he who abides in love abides in God, and God in him."

1 John 4:18,19 "There is no fear in love; but perfect love casts out fear, because fear involves torment. But he who fears has not been made perfect in love. We love Him because He first loved us."

1 John 5:3 "For this is the love of God, that we keep His commandments. And His commandments are not burdensome."

CHAPTER 1 CREATION AND WHY WE EXIST

Isaiah 43:7; Genesis 1:1-4; Colossians 1:16,17; Genesis 1:5; Isaiah 45:12; John 1:1-5;

CHAPTER 2 MIRACLES

Isaiah 55:10,11; Romans 1:20; Psalm 104:24; Psalm 40:5; Ecclesiastes 3:1; Genesis 1:29,30; Genesis 1:27; Genesis 2:16; Isaiah 44:24; John 14:6; 2Timothy 3:15

CHAPTER 3 SIN AND THE FALL OF MANKIND

John12:40; Isaiah 6:9,10; Proverbs 6:16-19; Mark 7:20-23; Romans 1:25; Matthew 12:30; Genesis 2:16,17; Genesis 3:1-5; Genesis 3:15; 1 John 2:4; Romans 1:28-32; Ezekiel 28:14-16; Isaiah 14:12-14; Luke 10:18; Ephesians 6:10-12; John 8:42,43; Deuteronomy 5:7-21; Matthew 6:24; James 4:8; Romans 3:9-18; Galatians 5:22;

Matthew 22:37-40; Deuteronomy 6:5; 1 Peter 3:5; Romans 8:5-7;
1 John 4:15-17

Chapter 4 Attributes of God

God is Self-Existing - Exodus 3:14; Acts 17:24,25; Job 41:11;
John 12:10; Colossians 1:16

God is Unchangeable – Malachi 3:6; James 1:17; Psalm 102:27;
Isaiah 46:9-11; Isaiah 43:10,11; Numbers 23:19; Hebrews 13:8

God is Self-Sufficient – John 5:26; Psalm 36:9

God is Omnipresent – Ephesians 4:6; Psalm 139:6-10; Jeremiah
23:23,24; Deuteronomy 10:14; Acts 17:28

God is Omniscient – 1John 3:20; Colossians 2:2,3; 1Corinthians
2:11-14; 1Corinthians 3:19,20; Job 5:13; Psalm 94:11

God is Omnipotent – Psalm 33:6-9; Hebrews 1:2,3; Proverbs
8:22-31; Isaiah 44:2; Isaiah 45:5,6; Isaiah 12:13; Isaiah 51:15,16

God is Faithful – Psalm 119:90; 2 Samuel 7:28; Deuteronomy
7:9; Deuteronomy 32:3-5; John 17:17

Goodness of God – Luke 18:19; Psalm 34:10; Genesis 1:31;
Romans 8:28; Romans 12:2; Galatians 6:9; Psalm 107:8,9; Psalm
106:1; Psalm 119:68; Psalm 84:11-

God is Love – Ephesians 1:4,5; John 3:16; Matthew 22:37-40;
(Appendix above)

God is Just and Righteous – Genesis 18:25; Isaiah 45:19; Romans 3:23-26

God's Mercy – Romans 9:15,16,18; Ephesians 2:4,5; Matthew 23:23; 2Corinthians 1:3

God's Grace – Ephesians 2:8-10; 1Peter 1:5

God is Holy – Matthew 5:48; 1Peter 1:15,16; 2Corinthians 7:1; 2Corinthians 6:16; Ezekiel 37:26

God is Peace – Romans 15:33; Romans 16:20; Ephesians 2:14,15; 1Thessalonians 5:23; John 14:27

God is Truth – John 14:6; John 17:17; Hebrews 6:18; Psalm 12:6; 1 John 5:20

CHAPTER 5 THE PRESENCE OF GOD

Revelation 21:3-7; Genesis 3:14,15; Matthew 24:35; Matthew 5:18; Galatians 2:20; John 7:37,38; Proverbs 20:27; Hebrews 4:12; Psalm 16:11

CHAPTER 6 GOD'S GLORY

Isaiah 43:7; Psalm 63:2,3; Psalm 57:5; Psalm 42:8; Luke 2:14; Isaiah 40:5; 1 Peter 4:11; 1 Corinthians 1:30,31; Ephesians 1:4-9; Ephesians 2:6

CHAPTER 7 CHARACTERISTICS TO LIVE BY

Isaiah 44:2; Isaiah 44:24; Ecclesiastes 1:9; John 14:6; Romans 12:2; Romans 12:9-21; 1 Corinthians 13:13; Matthew 22:37-40; Proverbs 8:13; Proverbs 3:7; Proverbs 16:6; Proverbs 16:17; Proverbs 4:24; Psalm 34:10; Romans 8:28; 2 Timothy 2:15; Matthew 12:35; Galatians 5:22; 2 Peter 1:7; John 5:23; Matthew 7:12; Proverbs 15:33; Hebrews 11:6; Proverbs 4:23; Proverbs 11:27; Psalm 23:6; Romans 5:5; Romans 15:13; 2 Thessalonians 5:16; Psalm 119:162; Luke 8:15; Matthew 28:20; Matthew 6:9-13; Psalm 23; Proverbs 21:2; James 4:10; Proverbs 3:34; James 1:19; Luke 23:34; Isaiah 9:6,7; Luke 2:14; John 16:33

CHAPTER 8 RELATIONSHIPS

Genesis 1:28; 1 John 1:19; Romans 9:39; Proverbs 3:5,6; John 8:32; Proverbs 8:34; Ephesians 1:6; Matthew 7:12; Proverbs 16:3; 1 Thessalonians 5:18; Ephesians 1:7; Proverbs 21:2; Proverbs 23:19

CHAPTER 9 WE REAP WHAT WE SOW

Hosea 10:12; Matthew 13:13; Matthew 13:19-23; Matthew 7:24; Galatians 6:8,9; 1 Corinthians 5:10; Jeremiah 17:5; Jeremiah 17:9,10; Proverbs 5:21,22; James 3:17,18

CHAPTER 10 SAVING FAITH

John 3:16; John 6:37; John 7:37; Matthew 11:28-30; John 1:12,13; John 3:3-8; Ephesians 2:5,8; Ephesians 3:16,17; Galatians 2:20; Romans 8:10

Chapter 11 Spiritual Growth

Psalm 43:3; James 4:8; Job 12:10; Psalm 104:30; Job 34:14,15; Acts 2:38; Romans 8:26; Ephesians 2:18; John 8:32; Psalm 37:4,5; Matthew 3:16; Psalm 46:10

Chapter 12 Treasures of The Heart

Genesis 1:27; Romans 8:39; Jeremiah 29:11; Proverbs 4:23; Colossians 4:14,15; Philippians 4:7; Matthew 22:37-39; Romans 10:8-10; Matthew 12:30; Matthew 15:18.19; James 3:14-16; 1 Peter 5:7; Isaiah 41:10,11; Jeremiah 17:9-10; Jeremiah 17:5; Psalm 37:3,4; Psalm 40:8; Isaiah 6:9,10; Romans 1:24; Matthew 4:10; Matthew 4:4; James 4:8

Chapter 13 Letting God into Your Life

Jeremiah 17:9,10; Romans 1:24; Isaiah 55:2,3; Proverbs 20:17; John 6:35; Luke 4:4; Romans 3:23; Romans 3:12: Romans 5:20,21; Ezekiel 33:11; 1 Timothy 2:4; Proverbs 4:23; Matthew 26:41; Ephesians 5:20; Isaiah 48:17; Psalm 43:3; James 1:5; Matthew 7:7,8; Isaiah 55:6; Psalm 34:4; Jeremiah 29:11-13; Proverbs 3:5,6; Philippians 4:13

Chapter 14 Hope

1 Corinthians 13:7,8,13; Jeremiah 29:11-13; Romans 5:5; Psalm 31:24; Psalm 33:18-22; Romans 8:24,25; Lamentations 3:21-26; Romans 15:4; Romans 15:13; Galatians 5:5; Hebrews 10:23

**Ted Stuckey is
Also owner and
operator of
LTC Christian
Apparel**

LTCchristianapparel.com

**Wear and Share
Your Love of
Christ !**